Contents

Acknowledgements

I would like to thank the following individuals who were generous with their time and ideas.

■ Annie Davy, education officer, early years, Oxfordshire, who arranged for me to visit two Oxford schools: Windale First School (thanks to Sharon Crockett, reception class teacher) and Grandpont Nursery School (thanks to Claire White, nursery teacher).

■ Ian Harris, principal road safety officer, for his experience and a copy of the Oxfordshire Road Safety video.

■ David Perkins, field officer for HAPA, for discussions about safety and risk assessment, especially relating to disabled children and young people.

■ Nikki Robinson, vocational training manager at The Henley College, for discussions about schools and nurseries.

■ Ruth Thomson, features editor of *Nursery world*, for the wide range of reaction to safety issues experienced through their postbag.

■ Gordon Woodall, Sally Pemberton and the team from the Forest School and Children's Centre at Bridgwater College, Somerset.

I am also grateful for the opinions expressed to me over the years by many children, young people, parents and a wide range of practitioners during individual conversations, group discussion and workshop explorations.

Notes about using this book

Too safe for their own good? includes lots of case studies and real examples from my own experience and that of other people. They are easy to find as they appear in a rounded grey box, like this one, and are intended to illustrate a point that has been made in the nearby text.

The book has several 'Think' icons like the one on the right. These mark places where I suggest that you think about a particular issue in the context of your own situation.

Introduction

Girls and boys need care and supervision throughout the years of childhood when they have a limited understanding of common risks in their immediate environment. There are real dangers to children from household or traffic accidents and considerable scope for responsible adults to reduce the level of preventable injuries and deaths. However, in an understandable concern to protect children from harm, have we gone too far in the opposite direction?

It is counter-productive to focus on keeping children away from every risk, however slight. We are likely to create a boring environment for them, without challenge or excitement. We also project an image of ourselves as people who block children's interests and curiosity. In many ways our society now separates childhood from adulthood and has disrupted the pattern of integrating children slowly into adult responsibilities and pursuits by letting them learn alongside us. And yet teenagers are regularly told to 'grow up' and not to be 'so silly' or 'irresponsible' when they have had limited experience of how to grow up or of what constitutes responsible behaviour in adult settings.

Our task as useful adults is to contribute towards children's development as they become competent adults, to be part of their growing up. Children need to learn about safety and handling risks, and adults have many useful skills to share with children in ways that are developmentally appropriate. You can also make explicit to children, through simple conversation, what actions you take to help keep them safe that would not yet be suitable for the children to handle themselves.

We need safety awareness and the valuable accident prevention work undertaken by organisations such as the Child Accident Prevention Trust. However, children will be poorly served if we do not also share the skills and information we have learned on our way to becoming responsible adults. It is not instructive simply to say, 'Watch out!' and 'Don't do that!'

The aim of this publication is to extend the practical debate much more towards adult involvement in children's learning. Workers and parents share the responsibility to teach children step by step how to keep themselves safe. Children's learning is a process lasting throughout the years of childhood and important lessons start in the very early years. You do not start and finish this task within a nursery or pre-school, not even within the time that children spend in primary school or an after-school club. In partnership with parents, early years workers are contributing to a longer process, lasting throughout childhood and to the brink of young adulthood.

The following checklist covers the most important general areas that people working with young children need to bear in mind when encouraging children to be safe in an active, enjoyable learning environment. All these main themes are covered in the book.

Checklist for ensuring safe, enjoyable play

- ■ Take the necessary steps, including a high level of adult alertness, to prevent those accidents that are preventable. However, your role does not start and end with avoidance of problems.
- ■ Organise your environment to encourage children to make choices. This will include an assessment of 'How do we do this to be safe?' or 'Is this the best way to do this?'
- ■ Focus on being part of the process of children's learning and be explicit with children and parents about how you promote not only safety but also children's learning to be safely competent.
- ■ Discuss issues within the team, so that you give a consistent message to children, parents and new members or volunteers in the team.
- ■ See your work in partnership with parents who will continue to have responsibility for the children long after your important, although temporary, responsibility has finished.
- ■ Everyone needs to remember the main goal: that children are enabled to move towards being competent and confident adults. If we have done a good job of sharing our grown-up skills, experience and insights with the current generation of children, they will have a model to use with the next one.

1 The truth about risk

The media

We need to give accurate safety messages to children, but adults themselves can become confused over the real levels of everyday risk, because of the particular emphasis within the media. Newspapers, radio and television programmes make daily decisions about what is newsworthy or which topics will develop into programmes that deliver the ratings for viewers or listeners. Safety and risk-related events become newsworthy at least partly because they are rare, as well as for any injury or drama involved.

In June 1998, the Child Accident Prevention Trust reported interviews with 450 children in a commissioned survey. Children aged seven to fourteen showed much more fear of 'stranger danger' than of being hurt in a road accident. This priority of risks reflected the expressed fears of their parents, so children and young people had learned from what they heard and saw their parents worry about. Yet, in terms of statistical levels of danger, this priority is the wrong way round. The nation's children are considerably more at risk from injury or death arising from a traffic accident than from strangers.

In England and Wales an extremely low number of children are abducted or killed by strangers, and the figures have not changed over the last few decades. Child deaths at the hands of a stranger rarely rise above single figures in a year. Although the death of any child is one too many, the figures have to be seen in context. For instance, in 1996 no more than ten children were killed by a stranger, but 270 children were killed on the roads and nearly 45,000 were injured. Road accident statistics are so common that they tend not to attract headlines, except in local newspapers, unless the accident is a multiple pile-up or the result of a bizarre set of events. By comparison, the abduction or murder of a child by a stranger brings extensive media coverage. Because it is a rare event, the media judge it to be newsworthy. However, in terms of danger from people, children remain statistically much more at risk from adults and young people whom they know – including members of their own family – than from strangers.

It is interesting to note that the level of child injury and death on the roads has not increased at the same rate as the level of traffic over the last few decades. Part of the explanation seems to be that parents have protected their children, often by taking them in the car where previous generations would have walked or cycled. Certainly, children are not allowed to play out as much as they once were. Other measures such as traffic calming schemes, improved road and car design have all exerted some effect.

Unfortunately, the side effect of parents' protective approach is that many children seem to be less physically robust and have restricted opportunities to learn important skills, such as how to cross a road. Ironically, it now appears that the pollution from traffic is more concentrated for the passengers inside a car than for pedestrians. The past few years have also seen an intermittent media emphasis blaming parents for 'wrapping children in cotton wool' and 'creating a generation of couch potatoes'. There is no protection from these blaming headlines and, with the exception of the more practical magazines for parents and early years workers, the media is often a poor source of sensible advice over safety.

Media-driven panic

Media emphasis on what can go wrong, given without accurate context of the genuine likelihood of danger, can seriously distort perceptions of risk held by parents and other carers. The following example of such distortion is described in full in *Swings and roundabouts*, Kate Moorcock's book about child safety in outdoor play.[1]

In the early 1980s, the television programme *That's life* ran a series of stories on playground surfacing, using emotive visual images of china plates falling from the top of climbing frames and smashing to pieces on the ground. Organisations who had long campaigned for the use of impact-absorbing surfaces were pleased about the resulting publicity. However, the dramatic 'potential death trap' approach (relatively common now with the many television consumer programmes) created a false image that serious head injuries were a regular event in children's playgrounds. Available statistics show that children in playgrounds often have minor bumps or scrapes, but major head injuries are very rare in such settings and always have been. Parents began to fear that playgrounds were by their nature seriously dangerous places.

Some commentators are warning of a similar pattern over the use

---

1 Moorcock, K. (1998) *Swings and roundabouts: the danger of safety in outdoor play environments*, Sheffield Hallam University Press.

of closed-circuit television systems (CCTV) in schools or nurseries. The existence of systems may cause parents to believe that nurseries and schools are more vulnerable than is really the case in most areas. Some settings have a genuine level of risk over intruders or vandalism, but this is not shared by all. (See also pages 60–61.)

Too many precautions

Any adults involved with children or young people should, of course, be concerned for their safety and wellbeing. They are bound, by law, to do so.[2] However, the management of safety should never be allowed to overrun a setting's primary goals, that focus on offering children many different opportunities to learn.

The increasing adult preoccupation with risk can create too much emphasis on removing every conceivable source of even minor risk. Letters pages in practical magazines, such as *Nursery world*, sometimes reflect what has been described as 'the precautionary principle', that we should always avoid risk where the outcome is uncertain. This approach is often accompanied by a tendency to speculate excessively on what can go wrong rather than on what children may learn. This precautionary approach is often brought about by adults' concern, understandable in some ways, that they will be blamed for any incident.

In the playwork field there is now concern that, while an over-cautious approach to risk-reduction makes for extremely safe playgrounds, it creates play areas with so little challenge that children vote with their feet and play outside the boundaries. In the early years field there is growing awareness that significant goals for children's learning will be undermined if valuable experiences, equipment and play materials are removed after one minor incident or because an adult voices concern about what 'might happen'. If adults insist on 'playing it safe', children may be less able to play well at all, and this will disrupt their learning and continued development.

The precautionary approach also assumes that it is somehow possible to achieve a situation in which there is zero risk. But no environment will ever be 100% safe. Even well-supervised children manage to hurt themselves, sometimes in unpredictable ways. Adults are responsible for avoiding preventable accidents, but a goal of zero risk is unrealistic. In fact, the precautionary approach itself entails a

---

2 Registration and inspection under the Children Act 1989 involves careful checks on health and safety issues relevant to children.

different kind of risk, that of an oppressive atmosphere for children. Adults who analyse every situation in terms of what could go wrong risk creating anxiety in some children and recklessness in others. Children who are fearful will be unable to learn and those who are more confident may have few ideas on how to handle risk because their play environment has been over-managed and sanitised.

Building confidence, not fear

The Forest School in Bridgwater was established following a visit in 1995 to Denmark, where forest schools have been an integral part of their nursery education since the 1980s. The goal is to introduce children to the natural world and to offer a real setting in which they can learn properly about use of tools, fire and their own safety. The Bridgwater team shares the reservations of other practitioners about a highly precautionary approach to safety. Unless adults provide relevant and interesting experiences for children, they lose the valuable window of opportunity to share practical lifeskills.

The Forest School has a carefully considered philosophy and methods, including a high adult:child ratio, training for all workers and an explicit approach to how children and young people will be enabled to learn. All the work aims at building children's self-esteem and their wish for independence. Trust is central: both the children's trust in the adult team and the adults' trust in the children and what they can do.

The Bridgwater team also value good communication with parents. This starts with information before the children's first visit and concludes with an invitation to join a camp at the end of their children's year of regular visits. (See also pages 38, 39 and 44.)

Risk assessment

Risk assessment is now part of standard practice for adventure playgrounds, and has much to offer other settings for children and young people. The key ideas are that responsible adults take a fully rounded approach to risk in the following ways.

■ Risks in any setting are carefully assessed through observation, discussion about and information on the frequency of actual incidents. A team should be aware of safety issues but also avoid swift knee-jerk reactions to visible hazards or the potential risk that they may present.

- There is a difference between a **hazard** and a **risk**. A hazard is a physical situation that could potentially offer harm. A risk is the probability that this hazard will be realised within an identifiable period of time and that someone will be harmed as a result. For example, a railway line running through an embankment close to a nursery might be viewed as a hazard. However, if the line is properly enclosed and trips to watch the trains are appropriately supervised, then the risk to children will be so low as to be effectively non-existent. The excitement of visits to watch the trains and children's learning from the experience can be fully explored.
- Risks are not absolutes, so it is important to identify the genuine level of risk, the likely consequences if something does go wrong and the seriousness of those consequences.
- If there is a high risk then steps may need to be taken to remove the hazard. For instance, a safe approach to hazardous domestic substances like bleach in settings with young children is to keep them in locked cupboards unless they are being used by adults. However, craft glue needs to be available to the children within a learning environment where they are shown how to use the material appropriately.

Acceptable and unacceptable risks

Some risks may be judged to be acceptable within the context of a setting and once active steps have been taken to make the environment safe and reduce the likelihood of harm. Additionally, children need opportunities to take acceptable risks in an environment that encourages them to push against the boundaries of their current abilities, to stretch their skills and confidence.

With this perspective, the existence of a level of acceptable risk in a setting is a positive feature and not a matter for regret or apology. Acceptable levels of risk, with supportive adult behaviour, can enable children to learn.

Other risks may be judged to be unacceptable and steps are taken to remove the hazard or make it effectively unattainable for the children. Steps need to be taken, but only as far as they are realistic and workable. Extreme measures for safety can become oppressive to children.

Staff teams need to understand and be ready to discuss acceptable and unacceptable risks in their setting and in relation to individual situations and children. A team that has a very long list of unacceptable risks may be over-protecting children in a way that will block their learning. They may then create a different unacceptable risk: that children will grow up unable to assess risk themselves.

A positive approach to unacceptable risk

A primary school in southwest London had two entrances. This made access easier for families and staff, but the school had a persistent problem with people walking through the playground as a short cut and using the children's toilets. Some outsiders became offensive when challenged.

Staff at the school weighed up the hazard posed by intruders, including the unpredictable behaviour of the few, against the wish to make the school welcoming to legitimate visitors. Children, and staff, were judged to be facing an unacceptable level of risk and a system was organised of locking one or both gates during the day, when children were neither arriving at nor leaving the school.

A letter was sent to parents explaining the situation and how the decision had been reached.

Using risk assessment

Risk assessment is a flexible approach. It needs to be responsive to:
- the main goals of your setting (if your policy and practice on risk stops the team achieving avowed goals with the children for your setting, you have probably created too many restrictions);
- the physical environment in which you work with children;
- the age, maturity and balance of ability and disability of individual children in your setting (steps may need to be taken for one or two children that would not appropriately be extended to the whole group); and
- observation and discussion within the team about how the current group of children use opportunities offered in the setting.

After unacceptable risks have been removed, a sensible approach to risk assessment often focuses on what adults do, rather than on buying specific equipment. There will be a range of options for adult support, help and appropriate intervention. Finance may also be an issue. The financial implications of dealing with a particular hazard will need to be considered, as well as the probability that an expensive approach will be the best way to address the issue.

2 From birth to eight:
what and how children learn about safety

Children learn about safety over several years. It grows along with their understanding of the world and of common patterns of cause and effect. People sometimes ask questions like: 'How old should children be before they are left alone at home?' But like so much of child development, there are no absolute ages by which children can be expected to understand given issues of safety. There are only general guidelines for what they are likely to be able to understand. So a more sensible and useful question would be: 'What do children need to have learned *before* they are left on their own?'

Whether in the family home, in early years or playwork settings or in schools, there is always room for informed judgement when deciding whether or not a child is able to deal with a particular risk. You have to know individual children, and apply that knowledge to a broader understanding of how children's ability to cope can extend over the months and years.

Children learn within a social and cultural context and this point is as true for learning safety and competence as any other aspect of their development. There can be differences between social and cultural groups on assessment of risk for children, and such judgements will affect boundaries determined by adults. Such differences can be subtle and, of course, there is a considerable amount of variation within given social or cultural groups as well as between them. Children's potential for learning can be shaped by adults' attitudes towards what it is appropriate to help them learn and what are the priorities in life.

Some social and cultural groups place a high value on helping children to learn skills that give them a role to play in family life. British cultural tradition has tended to move towards viewing childhood as a separate time, with the resulting problems of deciding when and how children are to move towards more grown-up competence and decision-making.

The following highlights of how children grow and learn about safety provide a basic guide to which you can apply your knowledge of individual children. They give some guidance as to appropriate adult responses and some broad advice about the sort of activities that might be safe for children at different points in their development.

Birth to one year

Babies have no understanding of safety and risk. They have neither the words nor the general experience to make any sense of adult warnings. Their motivation to use their growing physical skills and an otherwise valuable curiosity will get them into danger unless they are closely and affectionately supervised with an alert eye and ear.

Safety equipment, such as stairgates and play materials with no small parts, contribute to a safe environment, but they are not enough on their own. Unless babies are safely asleep or resting in their cot, you should be able to see and hear them easily. Avoid the temptation to think that safety equipment will do your job for you.

Never slap babies' hands, even if they are very persistent. It is an unjust action, as babies do not understand the danger you are concerned about and a slap, however mild it seems to you, will not help a child to learn. (Nurseries and other group settings should have a non-negotiable policy that staff never hit children.) Say a gentle 'No', but offer something else. Remove children's hands, again and again if necessary. Child-oriented settings will have very few items within a child's reach that are unsuitable for play. In the home, young children may need to be encouraged away from the real telephone with a pretend one of their own, or distracted from interest in the dog's ball to their own brightly coloured version.

Could things which interest very young children lead them into danger, especially in a home setting? If the answer is yes, rather than completely avoiding these objects or activities, think about how to satisfy the children's curiosity or their wish to hold and feel something by using objects that are safe.

Is what the child wants really unsafe or are you taking it away because the object is not a 'real toy'? If the object interests the child, and is safe, why can't they hold it and examine it?

One to two years

During the second year of life, very young children gain a great deal of experience in familiar settings. They build up the physical experience of what they can do and some grasp of what leads to tumbles, but there are limits.

Individual experiences of falls or bangs are not necessarily translated into an understanding that something is unsafe. It is *very* important that adults do not get cross with children who seem to put themselves at risk.

One reason for toddlers' apparent lack of learning is that they can be so absorbed in what they want to do that they forget the lessons of past experience. For example, two-year-old Kieran likes sitting under the table; it is his hideaway. If he sits there until he has finished his game, he usually remembers to come out on all fours. But today, Kieran's attention is caught by the arrival of the family cat in his line of vision. He says 'Cat!' excitedly, stands up and bangs his head on the underside of the table.

Another reason for apparently avoidable bangs is that toddlers have not yet reached a stage of thinking that allows general ideas to emerge from a single experience. They have no reason to think that the same accident may happen again and they also have only a limited idea of cause and effect. So toddlers often do not understand why and how they got hurt until adults explain to them patiently, and often several times.

Toddlers can begin to understand that some household items are not for them to touch. You can also help them learn how to distinguish between objects that are:

- entirely for their use;
- to be used by them only with adult help; and
- definitely only for adults to use.

For instance, while the big scissors are only for Mummy or Daddy to use, the small blunt-ended scissors are entirely for the child's use.

You can explain to toddlers that 'this is too high/too sharp/too hot for you', but offer an alternative such as, 'but you can watch me', 'you can hold this for me' or 'you can have this instead'.

Toddlers can plan and think ahead but they have a limited grasp of

Toddlers and new experiences

I recall encouraging my two-year-old daughter to put her hands out if she felt she was about to trip (especially important given the many uneven paving stones in our neighbourhood). Tanith followed my advice but was then surprised and distressed that she hurt her hands. As an adult, I had been most concerned about her banging her head. So I had overlooked a warning that putting out your hands only breaks the fall, it does not stop all the hurt.

Such mistakes are nobody's fault, and often will not be completely avoided, but are a reminder to try to look through children's eyes.

- *Do you have any similar examples?*
- *What did they teach you about the understanding of very young children?*

adult words about risk and of cause and effect. The concepts that they 'might' hurt themselves or 'if' they do something 'then' they will get hurt may not have any real meaning for them. They may also misunderstand a safety suggestion because you are unclear.

Toddlers combine considerable physical mobility and agility with large reserves of curiosity and a wish to explore. So they need safe ways to explore, a safe position from which to watch interesting adult activities that are not yet possible for them, and simple words from adults who realise that the safety lessons have only just started.

Three to five years

Between three and five years, children gain a tremendous range of experience and their ability to apply what they have learned grows.

By this time, children's physical skills have developed. They are increasingly able to understand and carry out ordinary tasks that require good hand–eye coordination and careful attention to what they are doing.

Within this age range, children will be ready to be trusted with some activities that were not possible when they were younger. Adults therefore need to monitor themselves on a regular basis. Are you still saying to a child: 'You're too little' or 'You can do that when you're older'? If so, are these comments still appropriate?

By this age, some differences can be clear between boys and girls, arising mainly from adult attitudes that have shaped children's social learning. In British culture, it is more likely that girls will be directed towards caution and boys allowed to take more risks. There is, of course, a great deal of variety within children of each sex as well as their parents. However, you may notice that at least some girls are overly careful that 'I might hurt myself', or might feel that some of the adventurous activities are only for the boys. The flipside of this process of socialisation is that boys who are by temperament more cautious may experience unfair pressure to push themselves beyond their current level of comfort.

Children's language has developed, in terms of their own speech and how far they understand what you say and explain. Children are also far more able to think ahead, to remember what you have told them on a previous occasion and to consider that something 'might' happen. They are able to benefit from information provided through your words combined with active demonstration, telling and showing.

However, adults must not over-estimate children's new abilities.

Children sometimes do not fully understand what you have explained, they sometimes forget the safety message and sometimes they just do not want to follow it. Adults also share this last point; how many times in the last month have you done something that you knew very well was not safe, like dash across the road to catch a bus or not look properly when using a sharp knife? Children are no more perfect than we are.

Children's social and emotional development is also highly relevant here. Young children gain immense satisfaction in learning how to do something new. Perhaps they are now 'big enough' to be shown how to carry the jar of strawberry jam safely from room to room. Children not only gain from new physical skills, their sense of self-worth is also boosted when they feel trusted to do something by an adult. Children become more confident through experiences that help them to feel

Three to four year olds and new experiences

Sometimes young children have gaps in their knowledge that adults can easily overlook. The summer that my daughter Tanith was nearly three, we had a day at the seaside. As she ran skipping towards one of the seawater pools we called out: 'Watch out Tanith, it's a rock pool.' But she did not know what we meant and ran into the pool, stubbing her toe on a rock. We were very sympathetic to her pain and showed her what we meant by a 'rock pool'. However, we also agreed that she did not understand because this was a new idea. Tanith recalled the incident several times that summer, she wanted to talk about it and have some more sympathy, which we gave.

Sometimes children are very literal in their understanding. Four-year-old Lenny was told not to run into the road after his favourite ball, which was a definite risk as he and his childminder walked

to pick up Lenny's older brother from primary school. He followed instructions and was safe on that occasion. But later that week, Lenny veered away from his minder and tried to run across the road in order to join his friend on the opposite pavement. Lenny had taken on board a specific warning about following his ball into the road, but had not understood more general ideas about the dangers from cars. His minder also realised that she had talked only about watching out for cars and so Lenny had ignored the bicycle ridden very fast which might have knocked him down if he had actually crossed the road.

Collect some similar examples of your own, from within the staff team at your setting, with fellow childminders or in a parents' group. What can you learn from the examples that will better enable you to help children?

think!

competent in their own social world.

As they gain experience, children in this age range develop a growing understanding of risk and danger. However, their perspective is still not that of an adult, and helpful guidance recognises this fact. You need to look through children's eyes for their perception of what is, or is not, dangerous if you are going to help them to learn. You will not always manage to see the world in the same way as individual children, so it is important to explain, sympathise or say you are sorry about anything you did not understand from a particular child's point of view.

Five to eight years

Children in this age group can be very competent in practical and lifeskills as long as they have been given opportunities to learn and practise. Experience is crucial, and neither skills nor knowledge simply appear with the passing of another birthday.

If they have been taught the relevant ideas and skills, children in this age range can have a broad understanding of risks and be able to take some sensible safety measures for themselves. However, there is still much to learn and some gaps in children's understanding. Children may genuinely not understand the limits to their skills. For instance, they know they can run fast, but do they know that they can't run fast enough to get out of the way of a speeding car?

Children all want some challenge and settings that are too safety-conscious can be boring. If given a choice, children may simply decide not attend this kind of setting. Otherwise they will tend to take one of two equally negative options, to:

■ sit about being bored by passive activities and learning very little; or
■ create some level of danger in the setting through their use of the play equipment, their created games or behaviour with each other.

Development is not only influenced by a child's age. An additional factor will always be individual temperament. Some children are by nature more cautious or more adventurous than others, and such individual differences will have been further shaped by their life experience to date. As much as children have learned, there will still be gaps in their knowledge which you may not notice unless you take the time to listen to children, especially when you and they have had a disagreement about safety issues. Conversations within your relationship with a child are just as important as clear safety rules. Sometimes they are more important.

Five to eight year olds and new experiences

During a family holiday when my son was eight years old, I was horrified to see him going down a steep, paved slope to a fast-flowing river. Out of my fear, I spoke crossly to him, saying what on earth did he think he was doing?

Drew's reaction was that he was moving down very carefully, which was true, and that he could swim, which was also true, so what was the problem? I explained my fears about him sliding on a slimy waterside, and that the river was deep and flowing so fast that he would be pulled away from the bank and dragged under. I said I was sorry I had shouted and that it came from worrying about him, then said would he please be careful.

Drew thought about my words for a while and then said: 'Well, sometimes I'm worried about you and you don't do what I ask.' I looked puzzled and he recalled an incident from a visit to the theme park earlier that year. Drew explained: 'I was frightened by the Dragon Ride and I didn't want you to go on it, but you all did and I had to wait and watch you.' The only answer to this fair remark was that I was very sorry that I had not listened properly to his worries and had made him feel dismissed in the theme park.

Older children will sometimes have comments to make about adults' safety behaviour or their own worries and we need to listen and respect children's views. Do you have any examples similar to Drew's experience?

Disabled children

Disabled children share much of the same experience as other children of the same age range. It is important that parents and other carers do not over-react to a child's disability or continuing health condition. It is understandable that adults can be concerned and keen to protect a disabled or very sick child. However, disabled children have the same motivation to learn and grow in competence as their peers, and adults should adjust no more than is really necessary in response to disability or illness.

The home or play and learning environment needs to be as safe as is appropriate for any children, allowing for their mobility skills and level of understanding.

Accessibility can be the main issue for children with physical disabilities, and this is an issue shared in some ways with their peers.

- Can all the children reach play materials, food or books without having to stretch or clamber in an unsafe way?
- Is the environment organised to create easy access and the opportunity to make choices between activities?

■ Are the working surfaces at the right level and can a child move easily in order to complete a task?

Disabled children should be enabled to move about and use materials and facilities, with the understanding that they will have some falls and spills, like any child.

Children with learning disabilities may need adult awareness that what is developmentally appropriate for a child may not be age-related. Depending on the kind and severity of a learning disability, children may need much simpler practice, finer steps of experience in order to learn, and longer periods of time at the different stages of learning than their peers. Perhaps there will always be a ceiling on their understanding and competence, but this must not be allowed to remain lower than necessary.

There may be some specific issues of protection from risks specific to a child's health or wellbeing. However, these issues need to be assessed on an individual basis and, as far as possible, discussed with the children themselves.

Adults need to develop good habits of talking with children about any safety issues. You should be able to voice clear reasons for not talking with a child, rather than assuming that, of course, safety is adults' business.

Disabled children need and deserve the same 'you can do it' approach, supported by the advice and encouragement that you should offer any child.

3 Dealing with incidents and accidents

However careful you are, however well-supervised the setting, there will inevitably be some accidents and near-misses. Children can learn lessons that are more positive than negative if you reflect carefully on your reactions:

■ what you say;
■ what you do; and
■ any broader consequences from an incident.

When adults are afraid something might happen

From an understandable concern for children, adults sometimes overstate the level of risk in what is simply an enjoyable activity as far as the children are concerned. Adults are tempted to shout 'Get off that wall, you'll break your neck!' or 'Don't run about with that lolly in your mouth, you'll choke to death!' Such exaggerated warnings and scare tactics usually backfire, especially if adults say them as a regular habit. Children no longer believe adults whose frequent dire predictions fail to come even close to true. Children also tend not to warm to adults who insist on always knowing better than the children.

It is a bad habit for adults to express safety concerns as absolute fact ('If you keep bouncing on the bed, you'll fall and hurt yourself') instead of possible risk. More confident children, or those whose enjoyment overcomes any concerns, will keep bouncing. If they do not fall, the adult then becomes less credible and more tedious. More wary children may take the message to heart, stop doing an activity they had enjoyed and perhaps lose a chance to grow in confidence and skills.

You will support children's learning more effectively if you do the following.

■ Avoid shouting at children. The only justification for calling out a loud warning is when you are at a distance and the child is genuinely in a risky situation. Even then, the danger of panic-stricken shouting by adults is that it often distracts a child's attention in a way that may put them more at risk.
■ Use calm words with useful verbal prompts like: 'Watch carefully where you put your feet' or 'Please sit and finish your lolly, then you can run about.' Young children need a calmly spoken 'No' and to have their hand or themselves gently removed from the risk area.
■ Reflect on your own reactions. Do you tend to leap in with a 'No,

you can't do that!' or 'Stop it right now!' before you have even considered the genuine level of danger? Have you developed bad habits in this way?

When something nearly happens

When something nearly happens to a child, responsible adults often experience an unpleasant mix of strong emotions. You may feel:
- fear for what could have happened and a sense of shock;
- guilt for your moment of inattention;
- frustration that your earlier safety warnings have been so easily forgotten by the child; or
- embarrassment because of the actual or possible reactions of onlookers, combined with a concern that, as the responsible adult, you may be criticised and blamed.

Adults are understandably shaken when they see a child nearly being hurt. However, what are children to make of common experiences such as the following incidents, all of which I observed in my neighbourhood over the last couple of years? What did the children really learn?
- A four-year-old girl rushed across the path of a swing in the play park, oblivious to the danger of its return and seeing only a gap to where she wanted to go. As she emerged safely, she was shaken by her distraught childminder who said: 'You stupid little girl! Don't you look where you're going? Don't you look at all!'
- A three year old walking close to, but not hand-in-hand with, his father stepped straight off the kerb as they reached a side road. The father grabbed the child and smacked him on the bottom saying: 'What have I told you about roads?' The child looked shocked and started to cry.
- A toddler wandered off in a large store and could not find her mother. The child looked perplexed and was soon close to tears. I saw both the toddler and parent and waved to the mother that her child was 'over here'. The mother came rushing over at speed, seized the child by the hand and dragged her off while shouting: 'You naughty girl! I've told you not to wander off. We'll go home now, no ice-cream for you!'

Some understandable feelings from the adult point of view regularly emerge as anger expressed towards the child, whose action has provoked the feelings but who cannot be held completely responsible. In the examples given, and in the many incidents that you may observe, the children cannot learn anything useful about safety and keeping themselves safe because any messages are lost in the adult's anger. Children may conclude that they are 'naughty' or 'stupid', and certainly that they have angered the adult. But they are so often left confused about what exactly they have done wrong, and certainly about what to do to be right next time. The adult's anger blurs the safety message and provokes emotions in the children that can actually block useful learning.

Children can only learn from a near-miss if you follow these guidelines.

- Remain as calm as possible and do not load your own emotions unfairly onto the child. Avoid cross words, blame or 'I told you so!' Certainly, never hit children and hurt them because they have avoided hurt or danger from another source.
- Treat the incident as a mistake on the part of the child, not as 'bad behaviour'. Children cannot learn from their mistakes if the experience is overwhelmed by negative feelings, distress because the adult is shouting or embarrassment at being criticised in front of other people.
- Explain your feelings simply to the child, especially if you have not managed to avoid shouting. You might say: 'I was scared for you' or 'I would be so upset if you were hurt.'
- Comfort a child who is upset, for instance if they were lost and you have now found each other again, or if they belatedly realise how close they came to being hurt.
- Explain the potential danger in simple terms, pointing out why the child's action was potentially dangerous or what they should do in a similar situation in the future. Taking the examples above, useful explanation of each potential danger might be to stop and show how the swing is only absent for a very short while before it comes back into the space with force; to look for opportunities very soon for road safety practice that will be appropriate to the child's age; or to make some practical plans about what a child should do if they get separated from you.
- Be ready to listen to older children's explanations or comments, including perhaps their view that they were not doing anything dangerous at all. (See, for instance, the example on page 19.)

When something happens

However hard you try, children will sometimes get hurt in your setting, although in a well-supervised environment, most of the incidents will be minor. However, the way that you handle events can offer more or less positive lessons to children. There is also the possibility that children's feelings about an accident that happened elsewhere may be voiced in your setting and you will have opportunities to offer support (see also pages 29–31).

Minor accidents in your setting

It is important to consider the common negative adult reactions when children have hurt themselves, when they have injured another child or when something else has gone wrong (see page 22). Here are some more positive approaches.

■ Stay calm so the children can feel confident that you are in control in a positive way. Let them observe a responsible adult model who moves in on the scene, checks out what has happened without adding to the panic or drama and who sets about helping any child who has been hurt.

■ You do not want a large interested audience and a hurt child may well want peace and breathing space. However, let children be a safe part of how you handle an incident. For instance, a close friend or sibling may want to sit beside or hold the hand of the child who is hurt. So long as the injured child is happy with the support, do not automatically direct other children away. Thank the friend or sibling afterwards for their help.

■ Explain what you are doing in terms of basic first aid for cuts or bruises. Explain that you need to clean the dirt out of a cut or that a cold compress will help a bang on the forehead. Be honest with them and do not say something will not hurt when it is likely to sting.

■ Listen to how the children feel and attend to what they say hurts them. It is disrespectful to children when adults dismiss children's words or pained expression with remarks like: 'You're making a fuss about nothing' or 'That didn't hurt!'

The aftermath of incidents

Some incidents will lead to a conversation between you and the children along the lines of: 'What happened here?' or 'What went wrong with…?' Avoid having this kind of conversation at the same time as dealing with hurt children. The presence of a newly injured child can make the whole situation fraught and you may jump to conclusions about what happened or even who is most at fault.

For incidents that merit a conversation:

- Talk calmly with any children who were involved. Show very clearly that you do not have preconceptions about who is likely to have been to blame.
- Invite comments and listen carefully, avoiding an atmosphere of cross-questioning. When there has been an incident, children are likely to see adult questions as an interrogation to assign blame, so you need to talk and act in a way that is clearly not judgmental. Over time, children will start to believe that you are honest when you say: 'I want to know what happened.'
- Consider any sensible consequences as a result of what you have learned. Individual children may need to learn about the results of

The banned milk crates

The children in a south London nursery class had a game that they developed with half a dozen plastic milk crates. They imagined the crates were cars and buses as they pushed them around on the hard surface of the outdoor play area and built enclosures with them. One afternoon, Daniel, a four-year-old boy, caught his hands between two crates pushed at speed and sustained minor cuts and bruising. A few days later, the nursery teacher announced that the crates had been removed forever: 'Because you can't play carefully with them.'

Daniel was upset because he felt somehow responsible for the end of an enjoyable activity. His mother was displeased because no member of staff had spoken with her at the end of the day about what had happened, especially when it emerged that her son's injury was apparently serious enough to justify a ban on the milk crates game. Furthermore, Daniel had explained the reason for his injured hands but did not say, as a teacher or nursery nurse could have done, that nursery policy was not to use antiseptic but only to run water over cuts and scrapes. The minor injury became slightly infected before Daniel's mother realised that he had not been given the first aid she automatically provided at home.

- *How might the situation have been better handled, from the perspective of Daniel and his friends who enjoyed the game with the milk crates?*
- *What were the issues in partnership between the nursery class and parents, in this case Daniel's mother?*

See 'The useful milk crates' on page 47 for a more positive approach to milk crates as a useful construction and play material.

their actions on themselves or others, or perhaps a play area needs adult involvement for effective supervision.

■ Acknowledge that children may have mixed feelings about an event. Even the child who was hurt may be distressed if other children receive a heavy punishment that seems out of all proportion with what happened. Children can also be put in a very uncomfortable position if their accident seems to have resulted in an absolute ban on an activity that everyone previously enjoyed.

You should also make the time to talk with a child's parents, even for minor bumps and scrapes. Explain what happened and how you handled it. Get across the message that the incident is now closed. You do not want a child reprimanded or even punished for being careless, nor do you want parents to tackle other children who were involved. (See also Chapter 9 about partnership with parents.)

Alternatives to bans

A sensible adult response to an accident, or series of related incidents, must of course include some thought about whether some changes in practice are needed. However, there can be serious negative consequences when adults respond with an absolute ban on an activity. The milk-crate ban in Daniel's nursery class (see box on page 25) is an example of a specific ban, but anecdotal evidence suggests that a fair number of nurseries and primary schools prohibit play activities such as football, games of tag and temporary crazes such as yo-yos in the playground at break time.

The apparent advantages to a ban on an activity or specific play item are that:

■ children cannot be injured through this activity if they are not allowed to do it; and

■ adults feel that they have made an effective response and workers may well have been under pressure from some parents to 'do something!'.

However, there are definite disadvantages to bans.

■ Children feel aggrieved, especially since bans are usually imposed without a proper discussion of alternatives. They are likely to feel that boring adults have stopped an activity important in their social world.

■ The opportunity has been lost to take a problem-solving approach with children and for them to learn through being involved in this process.

■ Many parents are increasingly unhappy about bans as a front-line approach to dealing with lively games or favourite play items for children.

Bans are usually only applied to activities or play materials that adults feel are optional or of little educational value. They tend not to consider bans when safety issues have been raised about activities or equipment that the adults regard as a legitimate part of the nursery or school day.

In a London primary school that I know, the staff team banned football and some pretend games fuelled by television programmes, and had no genuine discussion with the children. However, an incident in which a boy threw a set of scissors directly at another child's face brought attention to the boy's behaviour and not to a ban on scissors. It would have been inappropriate to ban scissors, but it was interesting that the team saw no inconsistency in their reactions to the different incidents.

As an alternative, a risk assessment orientation (see pages 10–12) can help a team to weigh up more calmly the nature of the hazard, the level of risk, the likelihood of repetition and ways of handling the risk. An additional approach, especially when children's games or play possessions are involved, is to invite the children's involvement in a problem-solving way.

The problem-solving approach

Adults have a responsibility for children in their setting, but all adults also have an obligation to consider the consequences of their own actions. An alternative to bans is to take a problem-solving approach that involves the children, and possibly parents as well, in a discussion about ways in which a game could continue without injury. Open discussion about a problem area in a nursery or school can be a productive way forward on a particular issue but can also have a more general positive effect on child–adult relations.

The basic steps in effective problem-solving are to:

1 enable a full discussion about the nature of the problem;
2 generate a range of possible solutions to the problem;
3 decide on the best solution out of those discussed;
4 put the proposed solution into action for long enough to see how it works; and
5 monitor and evaluate the situation, and discuss again as necessary.

Such discussions with children only work if adults give their time and attention. Children of any age are unimpressed with adults (workers or parents) who claim to want to hear the children's ideas, but then obviously fail to listen and still push through their own favourite adult solution. This principle is integral to any consultation with children and young people, otherwise the activity is not authentic.

Step 1: Full discussion of the problem
A proper discussion allows everyone to voice their views without interruption, name-calling or other put-downs from either the adults or the children. Adults can set the scene by establishing basic ground rules for discussion with the children. These should include:
- listen;
- don't interrupt; and
- no put-downs.

The adults have a major responsibility to model good listening behaviour, especially if there is no previous tradition of listening and problem-solving in the setting. You will establish good communication ground rules over time.

Adults can explain to children, or to child class representatives in a school council, how they see the problem. It is important that they voice their concerns with descriptive comments such as: 'I'm worried about children being hit by yo-yos' rather than put-downs like: 'You're all so careless.' Adults may also express general concerns about fairness, for instance that the football game seems to take up a disproportionate amount of space in the playground.

However, adults must then listen, without arguing or interrupting, to the children's perspective on the situation. It is the adults' responsibility to work to understand and show that they have grasped the children's perspectives. Make sure that all the perspectives on the problem are heard and probably written down:
- perhaps the football players say that the playground offers their only chance to play the game;
- some children may feel harassed by the energetic activity of the footballers;
- the main complaint of other boys or girls may be frustration that the informal football team is a clique who will not let other children join the game.

Avoid talking about possible solutions before the problem has been thoroughly discussed.

Steps 2 and 3: Choosing a solution from a range of possibles
- Encourage the children to contribute possible solutions to a problem and ensure that all ideas for tackling the problem – whether

generated by child or adult – are given a proper hearing.

■ Look at the range of solutions in terms of how each might work and what would be important if this solution is to work.

■ Let the children see that you give equal consideration to their ideas as to your own. You can be honest about your responsibilities and any issues that are non-negotiable in your setting, as well as where there is genuine room for manoeuvre.

■ Come to some level of agreement about which solution will be tried.

■ Agree on the specific responsibilities of both adults and children if everyone is to give this solution its best chance and set a reasonable time deadline for talking again.

■ Write a letter to parents, if this seems useful, explaining the situation and what is being done. Some written communication will be wise when parents have expressed concern about the problem in one way or another.

Steps 4 and 5: Action, monitoring and evaluation

■ Keep your part of the bargain as an adult and ensure that your colleagues do likewise. Children will not trust you again if you go back on your word or dismiss the new system at the first sign of a minor difficulty.

■ Monitor how the activity is developing from different perspectives of adults and children who are both involved and not involved in the problem and/or the solution.

■ Talk again with the children, or class representatives, to evaluate whether the activity is now going ahead in a safer and fairer way for all concerned. If there are continuing problems, discuss possible solutions.

Emotional support for children after accidents

An over-emphasis on policy guidelines and risk-avoidance can have the unfortunate effect of distracting adult attention and support from children who have been hurt or frightened by a near-miss. Children want emotional support, and anecdotal and research evidence suggests that their needs are often overlooked.

Even well-run settings may experience a serious accident. It is also possible that children will experience or witness a serious accident outside your setting and that their feelings and reactions will spill over into their time with you. Here are some examples of the sort of accidents that children could experience in or around even the best-run settings:

- In a carefully organised trip with the children, the coach is involved in a traffic accident. Nobody is seriously hurt but the children are distressed by the event itself and the hours spent in the Accident and Emergency Department.
- A child in your pre-school is burned in a scalding incident at home. He returns to your setting and has visible scars that the other children notice and comment upon.
- Your setting has an intruder whom you manage to persuade to leave the grounds but not before he has knocked over some equipment and been verbally very aggressive to both adults and children.

Adults are sometimes uncertain about how to handle the aftermath of incidents like these. There can also be considerable resistance to giving the children an opportunity to talk on the grounds that 'they will only get upset all over again, so it's better to leave it'. Adults who are confused about how to handle the situation may decide that supportive conversation is best left to 'experts'. They may also conveniently convince themselves that children do not feel experiences in the same way as adults and that 'children soon forget'.

A research project by the Child Accident Prevention Trust (CAPT) has shown how much children need emotional support after accidents and how often this need fails to be met, especially if children's physical injuries are minor.[3] Children who have witnessed an accident in which a friend or sibling was injured can be very distressed, but their emotions might be overlooked because they were not actually hurt themselves. In all these situations, children need adults who will take the following approaches.

- Listen to the children and let them talk as and when they wish. Neither children, nor adults for that matter, should be offered support at only one particular time (which is perhaps convenient for the relevant services). Certainly, a request for more support later on should never be ignored.
- Respect children's feelings and understand that some effects of accidents or of being a witness to an accident last for months and not just days.
- Let children judge whether it is more upsetting to talk or to remain silent. It is for the children themselves to judge whether they feel they have 'got over it'.

---

3 CAPT have published a set of booklets called *Getting over an accident* from their research project, which cover similar information and advice. They are adjusted for professionals, parents and other carers and for children themselves of different ages.

- Be guided by the children over what they find distressing and why. For instance, children may feel that an injury resulting from a game or sports activity is not a source of distress because 'these things happen'. On the other hand, a less serious physical injury sustained in a road accident may be far more upsetting to children because of their complete lack of control over the circumstances.
- Find out what children feel will help them, rather than assuming that adults know best. For instance, a child who has handled an accident with bravery and fortitude may not want public recognition or a 'certificate of merit'. Ask children how they feel before organising a public event that seems like a good idea to adults. The children may prefer to be treated completely normally, apart from having easy access to time and attention from a caring adult who will listen when they want to talk.

4 Learning from adults' experience

The development of British cultural tradition in the second half of the twentieth century tended more and more to locate children's learning within formal settings such as school. Concern over areas such as general lifeskills or road safety frequently bring the cry of 'what are schools doing about it?', when it would be equally appropriate to ask what parents and other key adults are doing about it.

The drawback to locating excessive responsibility in the educational system is that it places an impossible burden on teachers. However, equally important is the fact that this approach takes away much of the possibility for children to learn bit by bit, in familiar situations, from adults who have emotional significance in their lives. Cultural and social groups that value family and kinship are more likely to value how children can learn informally from parents and other familiar adults.

The ideas in this section are applicable to all adults close enough to share their skills with children, not only parents and certainly not only adults with a specific educational role. The final goal of childhood is to emerge as a competent and confident adult. So the current generation of adults needs to consider how best to share their grown-up skills, experience and insights with the current generation of children.

Step-by-step coaching

The word 'coaching' has traditionally been used in connection with sporting activities, but it has been increasingly applied in the world of adult work to a relationship in which one team member helps another.

A coaching relationship is one in which:

- one person, who is more experienced in an area, sets out to share a specific skill with another person to the point where that other person is then able to act unaided;
- the person doing the coaching is not better at everything than the less-experienced partner, they simply have specific expertise in this area;
- the coach encourages and enables the other person to do something that they could not do before, or to do it better; and
- the coach enables someone to learn step by step and to practise safely without over-stretching or provoking a level of anxiety that will inhibit learning.

Coaching is a positive framework for approaching how adults can support children's learning of any lifeskills, especially those in which there are safety implications. The idea of coaching children is also positive because it locates adult expertise in specific areas rather than depending on an image of adults who always know more than the children. As girls and boys grow older, they soon have areas of expertise, knowledge and specific skills that they can share, in their turn, with adults in their life. The relationship of coaching, skill-sharing and exchange of knowledge can become a pleasurable two-way process.

Tell-show-do

The essence of coaching, so that children can learn as well as possible, has been summed up as 'tell-show-do'.

■ *Tell* children what you are doing and explain why, as and when this is appropriate. Describe your actions in words and phrases that are simple enough for these children. Be prepared to explain again or several times, if necessary.

■ *Show* children clearly what you mean through demonstration. Children need to see how to do something and be able to make a clear link between what you say and do.

■ Give children an opportunity to *do* it themselves, as soon as you have completed 'tell' and 'show'. Encourage them to ask for help as and when they want. Offer guidance as they wish.

Let children have plenty of active practice and handle any mistakes with good humour and understanding. For many skills this practice will be graded step by step, and children will move on to more challenging skills as they get older.

Repeat the sequence in response to what children need and their own personal requirements for more explanation, demonstration or guided practice.

Offering help

Children learn best when they feel able to ask for help, confident that adults will be a genuinely helpful resource.

You will be helpful if you respond to children's requests as promptly as possible and in the way that they ask. Sometimes they may want physical help in managing something too heavy for them. On other occasions they may appreciate information on how to do something.

Children do not find it helpful when adults imply 'you ought to know how to do this by now' or use similar put-downs. Perhaps a child has been given explanations or demonstrations before, but is still confused, has trouble listening or remembering, lacks confidence or just wants you to go through it again.

Nevertheless, neither children nor adults find forced 'help' genuinely helpful. If in doubt ask children: 'Can I help?' or 'How can I help you?' rather than assuming that, as an adult you must know what they need. You can sometimes help by encouraging a child to think through a plan or possibilities, but do not always insist on children's working it out for themselves.

When there is a real safety issue, you may need to offer a firm suggestion but this can still be done in a respectful way to children.

Encouragement and constructive feedback

Like any learning within their lives, children will gain in skills and satisfaction far more effectively if adults offer plenty of encouragement with constructive and accurate feedback. Children are encouraged by adult input that takes the following approaches.

■ Acknowledgement of children's efforts that does not always focus on the end-product. Children learn from 'well done' for what they have managed so far, as this acknowledges the fact that they had the sense to come and ask for more help and another explanation.

■ Warm words of encouragement help a child to persevere or to try another method. You might say: 'You've done really well so far, let's see how you've got stuck here' or 'I can see you're frustrated, let's see if it will work this way.'

■ Children are also encouraged by appropriate compliments from adults such as: 'I'm so pleased I can trust you all to do this on your own' or 'That's worked so well. I wouldn't have thought of doing it this way.'

■ Constructive feedback works alongside encouragement by providing honest and accurate information to the children. Children do not benefit from being given indiscriminate praise or being told something is 'fine' when it is not. When children realise that things have not gone right, but an adult is still saying 'lovely', then the child loses confidence in that adult's judgement.

Sharing your skills

Useful adults remember what it was like not to know how to do something that now seems so obvious. The steps and techniques have become automatic to you, but you once had to learn them. You were not born knowing how to sew without stabbing your finger nor how to connect the right wire to the right bit of the plug.

Awareness of what you do

You will be a better coach for children if you become aware of how you approach and carry out simple everyday tasks. A basic task analysis makes clear what you do, how you do it and the reasons why you do it this way rather than some other way.

■ How do you plan for a task? Is there a sensible order of steps in how to begin a cooking activity? If you are going to mend a torn book, are there some materials or preparations that have to come first or else nothing will work properly?

■ Be ready to break down a task into steps that are as fine or basic as the children need. Young children or those with learning disabilities may need finer steps than others so that they can learn and find satisfaction.

■ What are your reasons for doing a task in a particular way? Why does this technique work better than another one? Do some techniques incur more risk than others?

Children should not have to fathom your reasons in a lengthy detecting process. Explain the 'how' and 'why' to children with a straightforward 'because' or through simple steps, like: 'You need to glue this bit first, then you fix it onto the other part' or 'You need to hold the bowl firmly or else it may tip.'

Be explicit about safety

Children can learn if you tell-show-do about any safety implications.

■ Tell children what you are doing and show them how you do it. Let the children do something that will involve them actively so they can learn. This active part may be that children watch very carefully at the outset, then move into careful practice through copying what you do.

■ Explain to the children when you are doing something to keep yourself safe. You might explain to children in words such as:
  – 'I need to watch carefully as I pour this water, because it's hot';
  – 'Do you see that I always strike the match away from myself. That's so I never get the flame close to my body'; or
  – 'It's important that I put my other hand here when I'm cutting

the sandwiches, otherwise I could cut myself.'

■ Emphasise the how and why of safety through question and answer sessions with children as individuals or in small groups (see the examples on pages 47 and 53).

■ Read instructions out loud, even for something that you personally know well. You can then alert children to the helpful role of instructions, for instance for a recipe, how to construct a model or how to make a telephone call from a public box. Children learn that checking how to do something is a sensible step. They will be able to use this route as well as ask for your help if they get confused. Your active use of reading material is also valuable in encouraging children to see literacy as a practical everyday skill and not just for school books and study.

■ Share useful tips and techniques in how to do a practical activity. Children can learn a great deal through discovery, but it is unhelpful to leave them to reinvent the wheel when there are tried and tested ways to undertake an activity. Good technique is also likely to be safer as well as leading to a more satisfying end-product for children. You might say: 'It works better if you do little sawing movements like this' or 'This kind of sewing goes up and down again into the material. It doesn't go over the side.'

■ Take opportunities as they arise to be explicit about safety, but don't overdo the message. You risk losing children's attention through excessive repetition or by harping on possible dangers like: 'I might burn myself' rather than practical approaches such as: 'This will work better if we...' or 'I've found this is a good way to...'

5 Self-care and caring for others

All settings offer plenty of opportunities for learning self-care and caring skills for children of all ages.

Care of babies and younger ones

In working with very young children, you may work with under-twos, in a nursery or as a nanny or childminder. You are primarily responsible for the care and safety of the younger ones, but you can also enable older children to understand more about the care of babies or toddlers. They are often very interested, want to help and are fascinated to reflect on the fact that they too were once so little and vulnerable.

Let the older children watch as you change or feed a baby. Talk about what you are doing and why, for instance: 'I need to clean Jasmin's bottom so she doesn't get sore' or 'We need to have Stevie's bottles extra-special clean because babies can get an upset stomach very easily.'

If you use disposable gloves to change babies, be ready to explain to the watching older child that: 'It makes sure that I don't pass any germs from me to Jasmin, or between the babies.' Perhaps explain further that babies can get ill easily if adults do not take good care.

As a nursery worker, childminder or nanny, you would never delegate changing or feeding to an older child; you remain the person who is responsible. However, an older child can look and learn, hand you the cream or a new nappy. Children are often good at keeping a baby amused, talking with the baby in the kind of repetitive pattern (infant-directed speech) that holds babies' attention, or stroking their hand. Children often like to choose a set of clothes when the baby needs a clean outfit.

Some boys and girls are interested to find out about babies and what they used to be like themselves.

Finding possibilities in your setting

It may seem more feasible to involve older children in this way if you work in a home setting, but at least consider the possibilities in a nursery or crèche. In a family setting it is very normal that older siblings can become safely involved in the care of younger ones, but children who spend a lot of time in age-grouped nurseries can lose out on this important area of experience.

Rather than saying 'We can't do that!', think about ways in which you could. Perhaps you can arrange visits by no more than one or two older children to the baby and toddler room. Or organise your days so that the younger ones in a nursery have some time with older boys and girls. Babies and toddlers also like and need the company of older children, so think carefully about how to organise this safely. Closer involvement of older with younger children might be part of a topic on 'myself' or 'growing up', but the activity is also part of valuable, normal interaction for children of different ages.

If the parents are used to you running a very age-segregated nursery, explain by letter and conversation why and how you are developing this side to children's learning.

Integrating children of different ages

Apart from their innovatory work with the Forest School (see page 10), the staff team of the Children's Centre at Bridgwater College continues to combine the best from the approaches traditionally known as 'care' and 'education'.

The team made the decision to encourage contact between babies and toddlers and the slightly older children. So, while the under-twos have an area of the centre that is especially organised for their needs, the three and four year olds can easily join them. A quiet room where babies, or other children, can sleep is also the location for peaceable activities such as exploratory play with a treasure basket or other collections of materials.

During my visit, I saw two four year olds entertaining a child under one year who was sitting in a low baby chair. The older children were talking with the baby and helping her to play with some suitable beads. One of the older children then helped the baby out of her bib and, with the support of an adult, out of the chair onto the ground to crawl. (Adults are always close by.) In the same general area, some older children were working with dough on a table and another baby crawled across. Supported by leaning against the adult's knee, this baby watched with interest and then started to squeeze some dough of his own.

Hygiene and cleanliness

Of course, it is your responsibility to maintain standards of hygiene and healthy conditions. However, children can learn about how to keep themselves healthy in basic ways. Young children may cooperate with what you ask because they like to please you. However, older children are more likely to continue with healthy habits if you have taken the trouble to explain why you follow certain procedures or ask the children to take a more hygienic option.

Keeping clean

You will wash the hands of babies and toddlers, but two year olds and three year olds are ready to wash their own hands, with reminders from you as necessary. A considerable number of food-poisoning incidents, both domestic and commercial, arise from contamination of food directly from adults who have not washed their hands after going to the toilet. So there is a very good reason to explain the importance of hand-washing to children, rather than risk leaving them with the impression that it is just one more thing about which grown-ups like to make a fuss.

Find a simple way to explain why it is important for everyone to wash their hands after going to the toilet and before handling food, either to eat a meal or to do some cooking together. First of all, explain about not getting 'dirt', 'dust' or other substances into everyone's food. Children can understand this idea because they can see sand, paint or play dough on their hands.

It is also worthwhile explaining the simple idea that some things are fine where they belong in our bodies, but that they can sometimes make us ill or cause some kind of trouble elsewhere. For instance, 'pee' and 'poo' (or whatever the children call them) are what is left

Letting children get grubby

It is possible to overdo the emphasis on hand-washing and general hygiene. If you are to get the children out and about and especially into the natural environment, then you will have to let them get temporarily grubby.

In the Bridgwater Forest School children and adults can get fairly messy by the end of the visit, especially after rain. Before every visit, adults check the woodland thoroughly for any hazards so that children can safely clamber, use the mud slides that develop in wet weather, gather wood and other natural materials, and sit on the ground for any activity they want including eating lunch. The team carry equipment with which to wipe children's hands if this is really necessary or for first aid. Otherwise, the practical view taken is that natural substances brush off and clothes or boots can be cleaned later.

over when your body has taken all the goodness out of your food. Your body needs to get rid of what is left, but the waste products are not dirty and neither is the child. However, pee and poo are a concentrated version of what your body does not want and cannot use. So, it is never a good idea to put it back into your body by sucking your fingers when you have not washed your hands, nor to pass it into the food that you or anybody else is going to eat.

The idea that some things are fine where they belong in your body is also a useful way to explain to little girls why they should wipe their bottom from front to back. You can explain that there are 'good things' that live in everyone's digestive system (you may use the more general 'tummy') that help to absorb the goodness from food. But that these can make you sore if they get into girls' vaginas (conditions like vaginal thrush). You may not address this issue in your setting or may discuss the practical issues with parents of girls. However, if you are going to give girls the important advice about direction of wiping, then you should be ready with an answer to their 'why?'

Germs and keeping well

The adult task is to help children develop an appropriate wariness about germs without making them feel unclean or frightened. Some general rules need to be communicated, so explain that:

- germs or 'bugs' can be easily passed on and make people ill – even a cold is not much fun to have and some illnesses are much worse;
- putting your hand in front of your mouth, for a sneeze or a cough, stops you shooting the germs straight out for someone else to breathe into their body; and
- for the same reason, everyone blows their nose into a tissue (rather than wiping it on their sleeve or the chair) and puts tissues in the bin.

Look for opportunities, especially if children make a relevant comment, to explain that not all health problems are 'catching'. Children with eczema and other skin irritations sometimes have to cope with their peers' belief that eczema is a kind of 'lergy' which can be passed on by contact. Until you explain, children may think that some other disabling conditions experienced by children are also contagious. Under these circumstances, children are not being intentionally cruel or foolish; they simply do not have the information base to know.

Hygiene and animals

A similar explanation about transfer of dirt or germs is also important if children are to play a safe part in the care of animals.

Explain carefully that children should wash their hands after cuddling or stroking the nursery rabbit or any pets in a home. Animals roll in the dirt or clean their fur after licking their bottom, and children do not want these bits to go into their own mouth.

The same care needs to be taken, and explained to children, if you visit special farms accessible to children or petting zoos.

Medicines

Guidelines on safety tend to focus on keeping medicines in a locked cabinet, rather like hazardous cleaning materials. This precaution is wise up to a point, so long as you also look for the opportunities to extend children's learning, rather than viewing the locked cabinet as the end of the matter throughout childhood.

If you work in a group setting, it may not be usual to give children medicines, unless these are regular medication taken by this child for a continuing health condition. Otherwise, it may be policy that children who are ill enough to need medicine should be at home. Childminders and nannies may be in the position of offering basic medicines with parents' permission.

Communicate a safe approach to medicines with children in the following ways.

- Read instructions out loud. Show the children that you check by reading instructions out loud, even if you are sure about the procedure and the dosage.
- Show how you get the proper measuring spoon.
- Explain that even 'good' medicines can make you ill if you take the wrong amount and do you no good if you take them unnecessarily.
- Stress that medicines are to help our bodies fight germs; they are neither drinks nor sweets.
- Take the same care with vitamins. Giving vitamin pills or drops may only be an issue in family-based work and the same principles apply. Show that you measure the vitamins carefully. Explain how vitamins are good for you in the right amounts but that too much is wasted by your body or can sometimes even make you ill (some vitamins have serious side effects in overdose levels). Your body needs just the right amount.
- Explain that special medicines taken by individual children are to

be used only by them. A bottle of medicine or a health aid (such as an inhaler) belongs only to a named child, to help him or her with a health condition.

Basic first aid

The prime responsibility for first aid rests with the adult, especially with under-fives. However, there are valuable opportunities to help young children understand what you do and why.

- Explain why you need to clean a cut or graze to remove dirt – that if you don't do this, an infection may result. Your words are particularly important because cleaning a cut is sometimes painful for the child, so you should be expressing sympathy along with the explanation of why you really need to do this.
- Splinters need to be taken out, again because of possible infection. It is also easier to get splinters out of the skin sooner rather than later.
- A cold compress on a bang can help to reduce the pain and bring the swelling down.
- Cold water is best for a burn or scald because it reduces the chance of blistering and scarring.
- If you use disposable gloves for first aid, explain that this is to avoid any exchange of germs, rather than letting children think that you are protecting yourself against them. (Disposable gloves in group settings are a protection for everyone and to ensure that children who have specific health conditions such as hepatitis are not singled out.)

It is good practice to show respect for children by telling them what you will do, rather than imposing first aid on their bodies as if they have no feelings. Listen to and sympathise with children and never tell them something 'doesn't hurt' when their words or expression says clearly that it does cause pain.

You can involve children in first aid and accident procedures in other safe ways.

- As children get older, ask them if they would like to clean their knee or work on a splinter if they wish, with your guidance. Older children may appreciate being given the choice as a signal that you trust them, but will often prefer that you do it anyway.
- Look for safe opportunities for children to help you if you need some first aid. Perhaps a child, who has washed her hands, as she knows is important, can hand you a plaster.

- Show that you follow children's advice, learned previously from what you told them. Perhaps a child will tell you to 'sit down and get that splinter out right now' or suggest that you sit quiet for a moment 'because you banged your head hard on that cupboard door'. You will show respect and confirm his learning by saying 'You're right' and following his advice. Adults who refuse to follow their own health and safety advice will undermine children's learning. No child is impressed by the message of 'Do what I say, never mind what I do!'
- If children are curious about an injury, answer their questions. Perhaps you will explain what happened to a child who asks how you got a cut, bruise or burn.
- Consider letting older children be a part of writing a note or report in your setting's accident book. Explain to younger children what you are doing, if they ask. If you let older children be involved, they will begin to understand your responsibility in the setting and can be assured that the accident book is not a record of who has been 'bad' or 'whose fault it was'.
- Try to make children a constructive part of the conversation that you need to have at the end of a day or session, when you explain a minor accident or injury to a parent. (See also the comments on page 67.)

Fire, heat and safety issues

Everyone needs to develop a healthy respect for and care around fire and heat. As with the rest of this book, this section is not attempting to downplay the risks for children from unsafe practices. Uncontrolled fire or heat pose a significant safety issue for both children and adults – many children are injured in burn or scald incidents in family homes and some are killed in house fires. However, there has been an unfortunate trend to remove any contact for children with heat or fire.

- Nursery and pre-school workers in highly child-oriented settings are often advised to restrict themselves to cold-cooking activities.
- Children make diva lamps for Diwali celebrations but never see them lit. Crinkled red paper is definitely not the same.
- I have heard an audible intake of breath in workshops where a participant has described learning activities with children where they have lit candles, for instance for Advent, on a birthday cake or for the pleasure of watching the soft light against the backdrop of a dark winter afternoon.

The risk of an excessive emphasis on removing all risk also removes potentially useful learning in any area. Children cannot possibly learn how to behave safely around sources of heat or flame if they never experience it during those earlier years, when they are likely to listen to your words of warning and advice on how to behave sensibly. Children who are excessively protected from understanding heat and fire may also become so intrigued that they will experiment in such a way that they create serious danger for themselves and others. They may be genuinely ignorant of the risks of an uncontrolled fire in dry woodland or indulge in dangerous behaviour, such as throwing inflammables like aerosols onto a bonfire. Children and young people may have had no chance to understand the consequences of their behaviour regarding fire.

I appreciate that fire and heat is a potentially sensitive issue and

Safe behaviour with fire

The team running the Forest School at Bridgwater (see also page 10) coach children in safe behaviour with fire over a period of months. Collecting suitable material for the bonfire, proper fire-lighting, safety close to the bonfire and cooking on the open fire are all steadily taught, even with their youngest visitors: three and four year olds from the children's centre.

The team teaches children about the potential danger of fire, but also how to treat this valuable resource with respect. All the children, young and older, are shown how to approach the fire carefully, to maintain a safe distance and to sit appropriately on the ring of logs set around the fire. The adults as well as the children always approach the fire from behind the log seats, then step over and sit down. The same pattern is followed in reverse when anyone leaves the fire area, whether or not the fire is burning at the time. Children learn how to cook snacks safely from the distance of held sticks and are part of the activity to find a stick that is 'this long' and 'this thick' (shown by adults). So, over a period of time, within the context of visits to the forest area, children hear practical explanations alongside demonstration and opportunities for active practice.

Apart from the evidence of how children have learned about fire within the forest itself, the team have at least one example of how this understanding generalised from the woodland experience. In one four year old's home, a burning coal fell from the living-room fire. The young boy calmly tipped a cup of water over the coal while the adults were still staring at it. When asked how he knew what to do, the boy just replied confidently, 'Oh, Forest School'.

you may need to talk carefully within your team if you are a nursery or pre-school worker. Childminders or nannies need to have a good-length conversation with parents about activities that are planned and a sensible level of careful supervision. However, we do children no favours if every possible contact with fire and heat is removed and no learning opportunities remain.

Fire and other emergency drills

Every early years, playwork or school setting needs a clear and well-understood procedure for unexpected emergencies. This procedure may be known as a fire drill, but in fact you might need to evacuate the building for other emergencies. Adults have a major responsibility, but safe evacuation will depend on the children's having learned what they have to do.

- Make children an active part of safety drills, such as fire practices. Help them to understand what you are all doing, how and why, rather than giving a sense that, in the event of a fire, adults do everything.
- Talk with children about the drill, explaining that it is one of those things that will probably never happen but it is good that everyone knows how to behave.
- Practise regularly and give children constructive feedback about what went well and what could be improved.
- Model calm and prompt behaviour, taking the practice drill seriously so that children will follow your example.

6 Physical play and exploration

Children need challenge and excitement. If their play environment is made too safe and sanitised, the children will either slump into uninspired and repetitive play or they will find some way to spice up their play environment, probably through energetic games or risky behaviour that adults do not like.

A safe enough environment

Every setting needs to consider the balance between safety and a decent challenge in physical play and exciting activities.

- Find alternatives to saying 'No'. Very young children and toddlers want and need to use their physical skills, so watch out for bad habits of adults saying 'No' without real consideration. You can keep very young children safe through appropriate and affectionate supervision, but also by playing enthusiastically with them.
- Ensure a soft or yielding surface for children's landing from leaps or somersaults. A low-impact surface in a play area can reduce bumps and bruises. Foam floor matting can be brought out for crawling-chasing games and safe wrestling activities with toddlers. In a family home, an old double-bed mattress can be ideal.
- Use natural opportunities to explore rules with the children for a situation that needs a bit of safe structure. Would everyone benefit from limits to how many children are on the climbing frame at a time or a system for waiting your turn on the rope in an adventure playground?
- Discuss alternatives with older children when there is unsafe use of appropriate equipment. See pages 27–29 for a discussion of the problem-solving approach.
- Explain safety rules whenever you are asked for details. For instance, you may always have a worker on top of the big slide because each child is offered help, if wished, to get onto their mat and the adult ensures that the previous child has cleared the bottom of the slide before the next child starts.

Learning to assess risk

It is important that children learn to assess and take manageable risks. Adults can take good care of children and still allow them some opportunities to decide on the risk level themselves, rather than always having an adult to say 'yes' or 'no'.

- Let the children say out loud how high they want to go and how they want you to help them. Children will learn about safe footing and judging a good jumping height. Your friendly involvement can empower a child to say 'No, I don't want to do that' or 'I don't want to go so high'.

- Support children's decisions unless you have a genuine basis for concern, in which case try a compromise with 'I'd be grateful if you'd try from here first' or 'How about you let me hold your hand first time round'.

- Make a clear and honest distinction between your adult fears and a child's fears. This may be the difference between saying: 'I'm concerned that it's a bit too high for you' rather than 'Don't you think that's too high for you' – to which the child's answer can fairly be 'No'.

- Talk about safety issues with children as sensible fellow human beings who happen to be younger than you (see 'The useful milk crates', below).

- Be ready to consider whether you, or other colleagues if you work in a team, are making different decisions about risk on the basis of gender. It may be that you are quicker to say 'Be careful' to a girl than to a boy. Alternatively, perhaps you are more likely to encourage a cautious boy to 'have a go!' and let a girl back down from a manageable risk.

The useful milk crates

During the morning of my visit to Grandpont Nursery School, the children had designed and built a channel to bring water from the outdoor tap to their sandpit. Lengths of firm plastic guttering had been supported by plastic milk crates in a plan discussed and put into practice entirely by the children without any adult suggestion or intervention. Having experienced another nursery that banned milk crates (see 'The banned milk crates', page 25) I asked Claire, the nursery teacher, how they handled the matter of the crates.

Claire explained that they discussed the issues with the children, for instance about the height of constructions with the crates. Staff are ready to talk with the children and demonstrate that, for instance: 'We don't climb on the crates if they are more than two high. Because it's very wobbly, like this...' She has since heard children involved in such constructions discussing with each other the features of their building and, for example, deciding that 'if we want to climb on them, we'll make it long and not high'.

Encouragement and extension

With some children the adult concern is to bring them more out of themselves and encourage them to try something different. You can help through a step-by-step approach and by showing respect for each child.

Explore the safe challenge zone for individual children and help them push their skills and confidence that little bit further. The support of an adult can encourage with 'Try it just that little bit higher/harder/longer' or 'Great! Do it again!' when a cautious child has finally plucked up the courage to climb or leap.

Positive feedback should be focused on the child. You say 'Well done' to a child who risked that little bit more, even if this was a small step compared with their peers. Never imply that you knew better, so why were they worried in the first place. If you respect the child and focus on their learning, you will avoid negative labels for children such as 'clumsy', 'nervous', 'anxious' or 'clingy'.

Assessing individual risk

The Hurtwood Adventure Playground Association (HAPA) starts from a commitment to the right of all children to play. Their London facility often takes children who have experienced difficulty in other play settings. The adventure playground especially offers play to disabled children, but is an inclusive setting in that siblings and local children can also attend.

A risk assessment is made for some individual children, starting with hazards that can arise from a child's disability (for instance frailty or likelihood of losing balance) or challenging behaviour (such as running off or eating inappropriate substances). The exact risk element is noted and the level of risk is assessed as significant, moderate or low. Plans are then made to manage the risk in such a way that the child is enabled to play and enjoy the setting. The management of the individual risk is sometimes related to specialist equipment, but more often is through appropriate staff support and attention within a high staff:child ration.

The staff team takes the view that experience of acceptable risk is a positive addition to the children's environment, not something to avoid, and that disabled children will have the normal tumbles of childhood.

1, 2, 3 – where are you?

The Forest School at Bridgwater approaches outdoor physical safety skills through step-by-step learning. As well as exploring the nature of the forest environment with children, the team supports learning about what to do if you have lost sight of your friends. They explain about how to call out or reply to the call of an adult of 'Where are you?'

Early in children's sequence of visits they all play the '1, 2, 3 – where are you?' game, in which the adults disappear in the nearby trees and bushes and the children have to find them. So the young children call out: '1, 2, 3 – where are you?' The hidden adults reply and the children find them from the sounds. Hiding and finding games continue as part of the woodland experience.

Children are allowed to go at their own pace. If they want to hold hands, then they can, but they do not *have* to hang on to friends or adults. When children are confident to move independently within the woodland, they are allowed to roam. The area is secure and bounded by a fence that the children explore in their first visits. Adults shadow children from a short distance so that no child is ever out of hearing or sight and children can easily get help or advice when they want.

Although some children have wanted to and enjoyed wandering off on their own, no child has ever got lost nor gone through the fence.

7 Practical lifeskills and use of tools

When undertaking any practical activity with young children, you make a balanced assessment of possible risks, determining sensible levels of supervision and a wise child:adult ratio for the activity. Many activities can be broken down into their separate steps so that children can learn safely. You can also talk about and show the useful safety tips and techniques as you share your experience and skill level.

Children have many years in which to learn all the skills that will support them as competent adults. However, even the youngest ones can be learning in small steps along the way. Children learn some skills fairly quickly. For other skills, you will want to monitor very carefully how much the children can manage and the extent to which you really need to be closely involved. There can and should be many opportunities for learning that lie between the two extremes of never allowing children to do anything that is remotely risky and handing over the electric drill along with the chip pan.

It is helpful to consider possible activities, even for the youngest children, along a continuing line of your decreasing involvement and the children's increasing ability to take responsibility. There are five general steps on this continuing line:

1 You do something entirely for the children and keep them away. Either they cannot be involved or you judge that it is not safe, however much the children want to help you by doing part of the activity.

2 You remain basically in charge of an activity, but you encourage the children to join in safely, in an agreed way and by watching and listening to you. You do not leave the children alone for even a moment. You thank them for their help or the pleasure of their company, however little you allowed them to do.

3 You encourage children to have a go and use skills that they have practised, but you remain very close by to offer help or advice as soon as a child asks.

4 You delegate a task to the children, trusting them to complete it without supervision. You are available if they want help but you do not watch over them closely. You are ready to check on the completed task, if appropriate, and to offer encouragement, feedback and any tips. Be pleased with them.

5 This task is completely within the children's area of responsibility. You neither remind nor ask them. However, you do take the time to compliment them and show that you are not taking their skills for granted.

You might like to bear these steps in mind as you look at the areas that follow. There is also an exercise on page 68.

Using tools

In many craft activities, real tools work better and so are safer in the end than 'safe', blunt child versions. Slightly smaller tools are sometimes easier for smaller hands and some adjustments may be necessary for physically disabled children to manipulate tools to their satisfaction.

Early years, playwork and school settings, who have addressed the learning issues involved in using tools, are consistent in saying that greater hazards can come from children trying to make inadequate tools work. Blunt knives, saws or scissors can be wielded with so much force to try to make them do the job, that even careful children can lose hold. Plastic rather than proper metal gardening tools often bend or even snap as children try to work the earth. Children's satisfaction is also greatly reduced when, despite their best efforts, they cannot produce what they wanted.

Learning to use tools is a process, like so many of the skills discussed in this publication, and not a one-off event. You help when you:

- show children how to hold and use a tool;
- demonstrate techniques to children in how best to make tools do the job;
- demonstrate and reinforce through conversation how to move around when carrying a tool;
- tell-show-do (see page 33) about responsible storage of tools, both how to put them down temporarily and how you store all tools in the setting; and
- decide if any tools are just for adults in your setting and give children your reasons.

Housecraft

Cooking Learning to cook is a valuable lifeskill as well as a potential source of great satisfaction to children, even very young children, who can be so proud of the biscuits or pizza dough that they have made.

By all means choose the simpler recipes to start with, but look for opportunities to make real food.

Share techniques with children such as weighing, cutting, spooning and pouring. Show them how to hold a knife and place their hands for safe cutting. Let them practise how to use a grater so that they do not scrape their fingers.

If you have children with you in a kitchen, explain and show how to deal safely with heat, including how you hold the handle of a pan and put on oven gloves, and give reasons why you do this.

Let children do as much as possible and then let them guide you and learn when you ask 'What should I do now?' (the answer might be 'Wash your hands'), or 'What's the matter with this?' (the answer might be 'Push the panhandles so that they do not stick out').

Find ways for children to be part of the tidying and washing up that completes a cooking or food preparation activity.

Access to the kitchen

Many nurseries or centres have a policy of not allowing children in the kitchen at all. Group settings are different from a home kitchen, as used by a parent, childminder or nanny. However, are there ways to help children understand something of safe behaviour in the kitchen?

- Can you arrange carefully supervised visits to the nursery kitchen at quiet times of the day?
- If you do most of the preparation outside the kitchen, can the cook organise to bake the scones or biscuits that the children made?
- Perhaps you can work jointly with parents who are willing to do cooking with their children at home.
- Offer pretend play exploration of cooking and safe use of the pretend kitchen for children to experiment with what to do and how.

In a family home, an excessive focus on keeping the children completely out of the kitchen can create its own risks. Young children may get themselves into trouble or simply create havoc if they are left in another room behind a shut door or a door gate. They are better with

Safe behaviour with crockery

Very young children need unbreakable cups and plates but three to five year olds are definitely ready to learn care with proper crockery and glasses which, after all, form part of the equipment of a normal home.

When I visited Grandpont Nursery School they had a museum corner where the display included china jugs. Earlier in the year the home corner ran as a pretend café and was equipped with proper crockery. The staff took time to talk with the children about the difference between plastic and china, which the children could of course see and feel. They all talked about being careful because china can break. There were no breakages while the café was running and the museum corner has remained safe and intact.

you in the kitchen, but sitting in a safe location. Can they sit at the kitchen table or safely at a breakfast bar, perhaps? Sometimes they could be doing something that is part of your domestic activity and at other times they might be happy with some drawing or play dough.

Galley kitchens can be especially awkward because there is very little room, so perhaps children could be sat safely at a little table or on the floor just outside.

Gardening

Children can enjoy the opportunities of gardening, and can learn about growth while learning appropriate use of tools. As with other practical activities, real tools work better for gardening and are therefore safer in the end than plastic or other 'child-safe' substitutes. You can talk with the children, as well as show them, how to use gardening tools effectively and in safety.

Safe behaviour with gardening tools

When I visited Windale First School, some of the reception class children were involved in gardening. One group was digging in potatoes and onions in the bed outside and another was potting seedlings in bought compost inside. Both of these activities were led by a parent who had chosen to spend the morning in the class.

At group time before lunch Sharon, the nursery teacher, took time to review some of the morning's activities. The gardening group was encouraged to talk about the tools they had used and to reflect in words with their peers on 'How do we carry our spade?' and to demonstrate to their peers 'How do we carry our fork?' Sharon confirmed their demonstration with: 'Yes we hold it down like this.' She then asked 'Do we run?' and the group called out: 'No, we walk.'

The children at Grandpont Nursery are also enabled to use proper tools when they work in their garden. Careful behaviour is again coached through conversation and demonstration. The discussion about use of garden rakes covers points like: 'We hold the rake like this. We never wave it around.' The practical guidance of 'We never let the rake come up higher than this' has also generalised and made sense to the children in how they handle their hockey sticks for a game.

Claire, the nursery teacher, stresses how this active involvement of the children helps them to understand the consequences of their behaviour in a very positive way, that what they do has an impact on other people. Children cannot gain this experience, nor confidence in tool use, if they spend all their time passively watching an adult using a tool.

Hygiene and gardening

Explain relevant hygiene issues, such as why everyone needs to wash their hands after a gardening session (see also page 40 about 'Germs and keeping well').

Unfortunately, some schools and nurseries experience problems with local dog owners who allow their animals to use the grounds and gardens as a dog toilet. It is appropriate that the staff clear up the results but explain to children what they are doing. It is possible that their sense of outrage expressed publicly might get back to these irresponsible owners. (One London nursery, with whom I worked some years ago, finally worked out that such people were physically lifting their dogs over the nursery wall to enable them to mess in the garden known to be used by young children.)

Construction, simple DIY and crafts

Three, four and five year olds are ready to learn practical crafts as well as have some involvement in simple mending activities that are part of the domestic routine of home or nursery. Real tools are safer in the long run and adult energy needs to be directed towards coaching children in a responsible approach to tools as well as some handy techniques. A wide range of arts, crafts, woodwork and needlework is possible in nurseries and schools.

Children can gain in confidence and satisfaction in both the process and the end product when they reach this stage. Organise your setting in such a way that children can find and use tools safely. Children will be able to locate what they want with written labels supported by pictures and tool boards with the outline shape of the tool to fit this particular hook.

Adults are important at the coaching stage and when you have children who are new to your setting. Never forget that your 'older' more experienced children learned the skills and techniques they now use with confidence. The coaching process has to start anew with each child as does the useful reminder to look carefully and 'watch what your hands are doing'.

Once you have children who understand how to behave with sewing materials or at the woodwork table, they probably will not need any closer supervision than for any other activity. If the children have learning or physical disabilities, adjust your level of supervision according to individual needs.

Encourage children to take their time with a construction project or craft activity and keep their projects safe for them to return to on later days. Ideally, there should be no pressure to finish everything in one session, although some work may have a naturally short run.

You can use group time to reinforce the messages in a way that children will find positive rather than nagging. For instance, you might invite children who have been sewing during the session to share what they have done and how they remembered the ground rules.

Be ready to talk through with parents what you do and how you enable children to learn. Conversations with parents may also help them to appreciate the process of their child's work and not just the impact of today's end-product. For instance, a child may have spent a considerable amount of the session hand-drilling holes in a piece of wood or redoing a piece of needlework to their own satisfaction. Apart from the efforts of the day, the child may also return to the project as a work in progress.

Safe use of construction tools

Grandpont Nursery School regularly finds that parents are most uneasy about the prospect of the real woodwork table that includes proper-sized hammers, pliers, a hand drill, saws, nails and sandpaper. The staff explain how they help children to learn and answer any questions from parents on their first visit and at the tea party for 'new' children. Children are shown carefully how to use the tools, handy techniques are shared (such as holding a nail with pliers and then hammering, if a child is uneasy) and children are welcome to start with soft wood before progressing to normal hardness. No child at the woodwork table has ever had more than an ordinary scrape or very minor graze.

The end of morning group time at Windale reception class included a chance for the sewing group to speak up (see page 53, where another talked about gardening). They answered the question 'When we're doing our sewing, what do we have to do?' with confident replies of 'Sit down; don't move about' and 'Watch our needle very carefully'. In Windale the larger and sharper scissors are just for adults and the children were well able to answer the question 'Who uses the special scissors?' with 'The big people' and 'An adult'.

During their Forest School sessions the children from Bridgwater Children's Centre are shown how to use knives, saws and tenon saws. They learn these skills over the months of their year of visits, understanding the best techniques and following the few safety rules. For instance, only adults carry the tenon saws from place to place.

8 Travelling around

Young children will always be with a responsible adult, but the time will come when they need reliable skills for independent travel. It is all too easy for adults to let the years, and the opportunities for learning, pass by. Then teenagers find themselves anxious because they lack any useful experience of how to plan a journey, keep track of landmarks or what to do if something goes wrong in the travel arrangements or if they get lost.

Young children can start to learn about safe local travel because you make them an active part of even short trips. Let them see and hear how you organise on their behalf. Children lose opportunities for learning when all trips are planned, run and navigated by adults. So plan your trips with child-focused timing:

■ think about what will interest them;
■ think about what the children might like to revisit;
■ be ready to stop and stare with them; and
■ make sure you are relaxed enough that children can actually enjoy and take part in the trip.

Local outings driven by adults' pace and interests tend to reduce children to passive onlookers and undermine these opportunities for learning.

Planning and navigating

When planning a local trip, you can share some of the organisation with children in the following ways.

■ Talk together in advance about the route you will take to the local market and what you will do and see. This conversation may be quite short with younger children, but they will then feel part of the forthcoming trip.

■ Four and five year olds may be ready for a short conversation along the lines of 'how shall we get there?' Children of this age have a limited ability to imagine even familiar journeys but they will learn with practice. The children can make the decision between alternative routes or the outward and the return journey. It might be that you will go out 'past the big building with the blue sign' and come back 'past Sasha's house because then we can go into the little park'.

■ During the trip, talk about which local landmarks you will soon pass. It may be the postbox 'where we post the nursery letters', the big tree 'where we sometimes see that black cat' or the baker's 'where we sometimes buy bread'. Young children enjoy the anticipation of 'soon we'll see...'

- Help children to focus on their surroundings by stopping at a corner or other decision point in the route and asking 'Which way do we go now?', to see if children can work it out. Young children will not yet understand the concepts of right and left, so make sure that you support your words with gestures that show as well as tell. For example, 'We turn left at the traffic lights and left is this way', using arm gestures as appropriate.
- Perhaps each local trip will have one or two 'child navigators' who guide the group, with discreet help, when necessary, from the adult.
- Over time, the children will join up their local 'mental maps' and you can help this process with comments like: 'Oh look, we've come out by the...' or 'Here we are, we walked to the market a different way today'.
- Older children in a nursery, pre-school or primary school may enjoy making a model layout of a familiar local route.

Using public transport

If you take a bus or train, use the opportunity to show children how this kind of travel works.

- Say that you need to buy a ticket if you are an adult or older child. Young children may go free on some transport, but explain that this concession does not continue forever.
- Show that you check the timetable or the map in the train for stops. Children are often interested in how many more stations or bus stops 'before it's our turn to get off' and they may like to count them down on their fingers.
- You can do some spotting of routes from the bus or train, perhaps seeing well-known landmarks from a very different angle. For example: 'Look, it's the common. It really is, it just looks different from the train.'

Finding each other

When out in the street, younger children should always be close to you – either in the buggy or holding your hand – and, depending on the situation, three to five year olds should be very close by if not necessarily always holding your hand. However, in safe and contained settings children can begin to learn about being a short distance from you and finding you once more.

For example, you might take a small group to visit your local library and spend time in the children's section. The children will need to spread out to look at and choose their books.

■ Explain to them that the whole group stays within this area and so will you. (Perhaps explain specifically that nobody goes beyond 'this door' or 'this display'.)

■ Move about giving assistance, where needed, and ensure that children can see and wave at you. Keep them in sight.

On a local trip with two or more adults, you could divide into small groups and plan to meet up later. Children can learn if you do the following.

■ Make clear arrangements between the adults, but in such a way that children can hear, be part of the plan and recognise an easy meeting landmark.

■ The individual adults can encourage children's active memory by asking before everyone meets up again: 'So, who remembers where we have to meet Sophie and Jon?' Adults can also ask who wants to be the 'navigator' to guide the small group back to the meeting place. Obviously, the route needs to be navigable by the child, so bear their age and experience in mind when planning it and give them such hints as they appreciate.

If you work with older children, for instance of primary school age, it will be usual to allow children to move around within a contained area, such as a museum display, small art gallery or enclosed city farm.

■ Talk through with the group where and when you will meet. Discuss this clearly as you all stand at the meeting place. Point out and involve the children in identifying useful landmarks to the meeting place. Make sure somebody in each small group or pair has a watch and somebody can tell the time.

■ Stress to children that you will never leave the given area without everyone.

■ Sometimes it also helps to point out the main desk and the uniformed staff of a museum or gallery, and to say that large buildings may have a tannoy system to bring together people who have temporarily mislaid each other.

Road safety

Road safety skills are learned over a matter of years and are the primary responsibility of parents, whose care stretches over the important period of childhood towards young adulthood. Neither nurseries nor schools should imply that they are relieving parents of this task. You will need to talk with any parents whose comments suggest that they believe you are, or ought to be, taking full responsibility for coaching children in road safety. This is an area in which it may help to develop different forms of communication, such as a letter, a display or posters and leaflets that are shared with parents in conjunction with conversation.

You can contribute to children's learning about road safety by homing in on those aspects of the process that they are likely to understand and be able to practise now. The most recent road safety research projects have usefully highlighted how children actually think and behave rather than how adults assume they operate. Road safety drills and codes have traditionally started with rules and principles for children and then expected them to apply the rules to specific kerbside experiences. In fact, children younger than eight or nine years of age most often operate the other way around. They learn as the result of specific, concrete experiences, from which they are then able, especially with the help of adults, to work out more general rules.

To help children learn about road safety, it is crucial to look through their eyes and from their height.

- Young children have difficulty in judging both speed and distance with the accuracy that is required to combine these judgements to whether it is, or is not, safe to cross before that vehicle in the distance.
- Traffic codes for children have often stressed that they should 'find a safe place to cross' but younger children do not understand the features that make a location safe or dangerous. They overlook the fact that they can be 'invisible' to drivers or cyclists, most dangerously if the child emerges from between two parked cars.
- Children sometimes judge wrongly that the shortest route between two points must be the safest or that safety is increased by running, because these choices reduce the time spent actually on the road. Children need plenty of safe and supported practice with adults to explore what is, and is not, a safe place to cross.
- Simple rules about judging when it is safe to cross have sometimes left out the message that you have to keep looking and listening as you cross. A car or bike may suddenly appear and some road users behave badly and do not stop, despite the fact that you are on a proper crossing. Children also need the habit of checking for themselves because situations can change swiftly, making it dangerous to follow a friend who started to cross when it was safe.

You will make a valuable contribution to road safety learning by taking the opportunities within local trips. You can keep your coaching short and to the point within each trip. Certainly do not try to 'do road safety' in a concentrated burst that risks boring children and will not ensure learning. Instead, use the following guidelines.

- Road safety is learned step by step with plenty of real kerbside practice appropriate to the children's age.
- Always follow the safety rules when you are with children, no matter how pressed you are for time.
- Make explicit what you do rather than always taking full charge in a way that does not enable children to learn from you. Even two and three year olds will learn to attend as you explain: 'We're waiting because some cars are coming' or 'I can hear a bus coming round that corner, can you?'
- Use a proper crossing whenever possible and alert children to the meaning of the 'green person' and 'red person'.
- When there is no crossing, show children how you find a place where you can all see what is coming. Four and five year olds will be ready to take part in a short discussion about 'Is this a safe place to cross?'
- Use simple rules of Stop-Look-Listen and keep listening and looking. Younger children will not understand 'look right and left', so focus on looking 'both ways' or 'this way and then this way'.

Concrete experience and plenty of safe, guided practice in real-life situations is key for children's learning about road safety. Stories, puppets or road-safety rhymes may support learning, as can talking about safety as it arises in the children's play with cars or roadways. However, this activity can help as a support but should never be a substitute for real practice.

Oxfordshire have produced a short booklet and video called *Footsteps: a parents' guide*. The material explains in words and shows in visual images how adults can steadily show children the elements of road safety and safely involve them in the process long before children will go out alone.[4]

Security and self-protection

There are three main themes to dealing with personal safety.

1 A safe balance in your setting between welcome access to parents and others who have legitimate reasons to visit, and security against inappropriate intruders.
2 Sufficient security so that children in your setting cannot wander off, get lost or make successful escape bids.
3 Ways to support children's continued learning about personal safety.

Nurseries and schools need sensible measures that neither turn the building and grounds into a fortress, nor create the impression for parents

---

4 If you are interested in this innovatory approach, contact the Oxfordshire Road Safety Group on 01865 815717.

or the children that there is a high level of danger when this is not the case.

■ Monitor who comes in and out of your setting so that people cannot simply wander in, nor children wander out, without somebody being immediately aware.

■ CCTV (see also pages 8–9) is not necessarily a sensible or viable option for every setting. Furthermore, technology does not do the security job for you without further adult energy and alertness. Even the best system still relies on sensible and consistent behaviour by adults.

■ The low-technology option that is crucial for all settings still involves taking effective steps to shut front doors, or intervening doors in some buildings, and having a reliable system to lock front gates to keep children safely inside. All adults, staff, parents and legitimate visitors share this important responsibility.

■ You need to judge your own area, both for the genuine risks of intruders and for vandalism. If you need to take steps, for instance to prevent break-ins and vandalism of nursery resources, then explain to the children why you have installed grilles on the windows or a burglar alarm system.

Teaching children about personal safety

There are several interrelated issues about the process of helping children to learn self-protection.

■ Children need to learn about keeping themselves as safe as possible without believing that it is all their responsibility. Adults are responsible for behaving properly and not putting children in an uncomfortable or difficult position. Adults should behave within the rules of fair and considerate behaviour.

■ Children should not be put at risk by otherwise well-meaning adults who impose blanket rules like 'You must be polite to adults' or 'Don't shout'. Some adults do not deserve politeness and some situations call for shouting.

■ Ways of approaching personal safety with children should not focus exclusively on 'stranger danger' (see also page 7). Children are not helped by an unrealistic view of the world that generates anxiety about dangers lurking behind every bush.

■ Another risk in focusing only on 'strangers' is that children soon regard an unknown or scarcely known person as safe if they are pleasant. Additionally, children are mostly ill-treated or abused by people they know.

■ A constructive approach to coaching children in self-protection includes children's rights over their own bodies and that there are

Turning a problem into a solution

A few children are keen escapees and can be very creative in their attempts. Apart from exploring possible reasons for the escape bids, a team has to be as alert as possible without oppressing a child.

Some years ago I was working with a day nursery that had an enthusiastic three-year-old escapee. Michael was adept at climbing the nursery fence and, on one occasion, managed to drag the ladder from the outdoor climbing frame to the fence and was nearly over when caught. The team worked very well together in an approach that combined alert supervision with avoidance of making a drama out of the escapes. Michael's key worker aimed to redirect his impressive planning and physical skills into activities within the setting. Within a few weeks, Michael had been helped to make friends and he no longer wanted to escape from a setting that he enjoyed.

The example also highlights the limits to a banning approach (see pages 25–27). The nursery team swiftly dismissed any idea of removing the ladder to the climbing frame and it was right that they did not, since such an action would have been unjust for the rest of the group.

private areas to anyone's body. Children need to be encouraged to tell about anything that concerns them, and should of course be reassured by a sympathetic and listening adult. The focus on telling can be linked with the idea that nobody has to keep a secret that makes them unhappy or uncomfortable.

■ Exploration of this area of safety with children should be done in partnership with parents and as part of a process that will stretch into older childhood. You will find more ideas in my book on child protection[5] and from the organisation Kidscape.

Another theme is that you can be honest about when you take any safety measure with the group. Children notice and are not frightened if you explain in a straightforward way, such as:

■ 'I brought us out of the post office because that woman was getting very angry and swearing. We'll go back later when she's gone'; or

■ 'Yes, I think that man was very drunk and he was getting silly and rude. We don't need that.'

Be prepared to talk about an uncomfortable or unpleasant incident if the children wish. They may also wish to play it out. In some cases you would judge that the parents should be told but in cases of minor unpleasantness this will usually not be necessary.

---

5 Lindon, J. (1998) *Child protection and early years work*, Hodder and Stoughton.

9 Partnership with parents

Whatever the setting in which you work, you are sharing responsibility with children's parents. The parents have a continuing responsibility stretching into the later childhood and young adulthood of their sons and daughters, and what you do should never imply that you are taking over that obligation. An effective partnership has many aspects, starting with first contacts.

Early contact with parents

Your first conversations with parents need to establish the atmosphere of a dialogue between families and the setting and this focus is as true for safety issues as any other aspect of your work.

- Make parents welcome to visit your setting before their child starts and offer a welcoming atmosphere in which it is easy for them to ask questions or to comment.
- Address broad safety issues in your written material and in any talks that you give to groups of parents. However, ensure that you ground the safety discussion in positive approaches of what children can learn and how you support their growing skills of self-reliance.
- In conversation with parents you will hear varied outlooks on risk and children's ability to learn. The family attitudes will be a blend of these individual parents and the social and cultural traditions that they have absorbed through their own childhood. Listen to what parents say and be ready to learn, as well as to explain the current approach in your setting or how you run home-based care as a childminder.
- Familiarise yourself with the varied attitudes in your local area and be careful about attributing the views of one or two parents to their social or cultural group, when they may be expressing more personal views. You are more at risk of this kind of generalisation when parents are from a different social or cultural group than you.
- Avoid communicating long lists of risks of which your team is aware. You may give parents the impression that your setting is a dangerous place. You want to communicate that your goal is to prevent the preventable accidents and then create an environment in which children can learn to manage risks appropriate to their developmental understanding.
- Your setting's health and safety policy should be easily available for parents to read, just as with any of your policies and procedures.

- Be ready to follow up any concerns through individual conversations with parents. Explain what you do, how and why rather than offering blanket 'Don't worry' reassurances.
- Show within conversation with parents that you are very ready to address particular issues about their children, demonstrating that you do take a genuinely individual approach. Some parents may wish to discuss what they see as their child's over-confidence that leads them into greater risk-taking whereas other parents may be looking for a supportive boost for their child whom they see as overly anxious.
- Parents of disabled children can be concerned for their child. You should be ready to address the individual needs of the child and not just a general disability label. Parents can be what outsiders describe as 'over-protective' of disabled sons and daughters and you need to respect the source of such feelings. However, the parents may just as likely be keen that you do not limit their child's play and learning experience out of a misplaced concern based in disability.

Continued communication in partnership

Keep the channels of communication open with parents through all the possible routes. These include:
- conversations with individual parents about what their child is doing in all the positive ways, not only when something has gone awry;
- displays of work, work in progress and the photographic displays that are often the best way to communicate the variety and depth of children's involvement;
- easy access to their children's work and records of developmental progress; and
- open sessions, days or meetings with a flexibility that can reflect parents' other obligations.

Conversations with parents can highlight what their children are learning and the progress they have made in handling tools or taking care before they jump down from the climbing frame. This discussion is an integral part of communication about children's development and would be linked to written records that you keep on all the children.

Displays and newsletters sent home can highlight particular aspects of your work with the children. You might explain the main topic that children are exploring over the next few weeks, including details about:

- the topic and its various aspects;
- what you hope the children will be enabled to learn – expressed in ordinary language;
- suggested ways in which parents could be part of the work in your setting or pick up on themes at home, if they wish; and
- specific skills that you would welcome if they are available in the parent group.

It is important to stress the shared nature of the work on some areas with safety implications. For instance, you may explicitly approach early road safety awareness through local trips with children (see for instance pages 58–60). However, make sure that there is no sense of 'we are teaching your children all about road safety'. This area should always be a shared task with parents and is definitely one on which they must feel an active partner, since learning about road safety is a process stretching into the future for all young children.

In many settings parents sign a general agreement form about regular local trips that are organised with the children. Less usual outings will need to be addressed through a specific agreement, covering:

- what you will do, how and where;
- what you hope the children will be enabled to learn;
- practical details about what children will need, including clothing;
- information on how you handle any safety aspects; and
- a welcome for parents to ask questions, with a contact person named if appropriate.

When there has been an incident

Most parents are reasonable people and it is crucial that a team does not develop, unchallenged, a negative view of the parent group based only on a few argumentative or cranky individuals. However, the most fair-minded parents will become irritated and uncooperative if they are treated with disrespect. A sense of inequality can arise because a team is careless about ensuring communication after an incident or when parents' anxieties are dismissed as fussing or overprotection.

You need a reliable system for ensuring communication with individual parents when their child has been involved in an accident. It may be this parent's child was the one hurt. However, parents may also need to know if their child was distressed by an accident experienced by a friend or if their child contributed to the circumstance leading to an accident. In the latter situation, it is important to stress that the conversation is 'for information only'. The child is not to be reprimanded or punished for a second time.

More general communication with parents can be appropriate when something has happened that affects many or all of the children. Perhaps a child from your setting has been injured or killed in a road accident. It is appropriate to send a letter to all the families explaining the situation and how you are approaching children's feelings and concerns.

Increasing willingness to sue?

It has to be recognised that taking legal steps after an accident has become more common in the UK than in previous decades. We have not yet reached the atmosphere prevalent in the United States, but some families are quick to threaten legal action if their child is hurt. You cannot completely avoid this risk but some steps reduce the likelihood.

- Make sure that all the responsible steps to ensure a safe environment are taken in your setting. None of the ideas in this publication encourage sloppiness over safety and careful supervision.
- Communicate clearly with parents from the outset about your approach to health and safety, both in general and in the specific steps you take with their child.
- Communicate honestly and promptly with parents when there has been an accident involving their child.
- Be ready to explore promptly within a team what happened, including whether the accident was realistically preventable and how the incident was handled. If there are lessons to learn, ensure that the appropriate steps are taken. Make sure that you have written up the incident promptly and fully.
- If parents are dissatisfied and threatening legal action, contact more senior people including your legal representative or department. Take their advice on how to proceed, including the nature of any further conversations with the parents.
- Sometimes the legal representative of an organisation or a local authority will decide that it is better to settle out of court than to fight a case. This decision can be made despite full confidence in what your team did and your general procedures. Such a decision may seem unfair to you, and unfortunately can encourage some families to try the legal route. However, settling out of court can be

seen as the cheaper and safer option when the outcome of a full court case seems uncertain. People and organisations who are proved free of blame in a court case can nevertheless still end up with a large legal bill because costs are not always assigned to the other side.

Meeting parents concerns with respect

Page 55 describes the careful approach by Grandpont Nursery in response to parents' usual wariness about the woodwork table, and page 10 the approach of the Bridgwater Forest School to clear communication with parents. Not all settings are so respectful towards parents, nor do all acknowledge that, as parents are naturally concerned about the wellbeing of their sons and daughters, their questions are not necessarily a challenge to nursery or school staff.

Parents are not reassured by blanket reassurances of the type that 'we are professionals, of course your children will be fine'. Parents reasonably want their safety questions answered courteously. I can recall my feelings when I asked the deputy head of my children's primary school whether the coach taking them on a three-day residential trip would be fitted with seat belts and was given a blunt 'No' in reply.

In another London school, questions from parents that related to children's safety in the unknown environment of an adventure holiday and the possibility of intruders were persistently answered only in terms of the children's possible actions and how staff were experienced in making sure that the children behaved properly.

10 Staff activities for ensuring safe, enjoyable play

Activity 1: steps along the way

Look at the everyday activities on the following page and decide where you are currently with the children in terms of the five learning steps that were described on page 50. Those steps are:

1 you do something entirely for the children;
2 you encourage the children to take part under your watchful eye;
3 you encourage the children to work on the task and you remain at a close distance;
4 you delegate a task to the children; and
5 the task is completely the children's responsibility.

If you work in a team, discuss your ideas with colleagues. Some items are more immediately relevant to a home setting than a nursery or pre-school, so if you work within a group consider how these items might be something to share with parents and check that children's experience is well-rounded. If you work as a childminder or a nanny, or are a parent, then you can consider directly what you do.

■ Look at any items where you think you and the children are at Step 1. Is there any way to help the children learn about this activity even though it is not yet time for hands-on experience?

■ Select four or five items and look for ways in which you could move on a step with the children. What will you do to help them with each individual item? Are there ways to involve or trust children to take more responsibility?

■ In your team discuss any items which you feel are 'not something we can do here at all'. At least discuss 'are we sure this is impossible, in any way?' and 'who exactly says we can't?'

Activity 2: risk and learning survey in your setting

Make an audit of the environment in which you work and spend time with children.

You might be an early years worker, a childminder caring for other people's children in your own home or a nanny with responsibility for children in their home environment. The idea is to look out for safety issues, but also to be alert for opportunities to extend children's level of

Everyday activity	Step 1	Step 2	Step 3	Step 4	Step 5
Going to the toilet alone					
Crossing the road on a pedestrian crossing					
Buying something in a shop					
Using needle and thread					
Changing the baby					
Locking up the building or setting the alarm					
Pouring a drink of juice for self or others					
Getting a cold drink from the fridge					
Laying the table, including cutlery					
Making a snack					
Using ordinary scissors					
Making a cup of tea or coffee					
Dressing without help					
Completing an entry in the setting's accident book					
Running a message for you from one room to another					
Tidying up toys					
Cleaning a cut					
Sitting with a book or toy alone in a room					
Washing up some cups					
Changing a light bulb or plug					
Operating the washing machine					
Getting plasters out of the medicine cabinet					
Lighting candles on a birthday cake or a diva lamp					
Posting letters					
Ironing					
Using short steps to get something off a higher shelf					
Answering the telephone					
Feeding pets					
Weeding in the garden					
Going alone to the local shop five minutes walk away					

competence, their understanding about risk and how to keep safe. Bear in mind that no environment can be made completely risk-free. Children, and adults, are capable of hurting themselves in the most unlikely ways, even in a carefully planned and managed safe environment.

You could make the following assessments.

■ Look carefully at different areas of the environment one at a time. (You might focus on the garden or outdoor area or on specific rooms such as the bathroom or the kitchen.)

■ Where and how do the safety issues arise?

■ What can you do to make an area as safe as is sensible so that children can still enjoy themselves? Look back at the discussion on risk assessment on pages 10–12.

■ How do you, and your colleagues if you have them, behave in order to keep the setting safe?

■ How do you show the children that you are keeping them safe, and in such a way that you neither worry nor irritate them and you help them to learn?

Put the safety issues into four broad categories:

1 This issue is completely an adult responsibility which you do not discuss with children at all (or perhaps discuss with them only under exceptional circumstances).

2 Something that is fully an adult responsibility, but you are careful to explain to children what you are doing and your reasons.

3 A safety issue that you introduce and explain as a shared responsibility with children. You monitor the situation and perhaps remind children about certain actions appropriately. However, you make the effort to trust them to take some of the responsibility to keep themselves and perhaps their peers safe.

4 Part of daily practice that has been delegated to the children. They can discuss the matter with you and you will help if problems or disagreements arise. However, the aim is to communicate that you trust the children to take care of themselves.

(For example, cleaning and disinfecting the toilets is an adult responsibility that should go in Category 1, and in which children are unlikely to be interested unless they ask about the cleaning materials that are locked away or the fragrance of some products. However, looking after pets can be an activity in which some parts are shared with children, such as ensuring the rabbit does not escape nor is run down by bicycles. It would therefore go in Category 3.)

Activity 3: supporting competence in safety through topic work

Raise and explore learning competence and safety in a natural way within the context of topic work with the children. Always look for a focus of what children can do and how, rather than an emphasis on 'don't' or on scary surveys of what can go wrong. Possible topics could include:

- our bodies;
- health and illness;
- food – growing, buying, preparing and cooking;
- transport, the local environment and travel; and
- the outdoors – plants and gardening, country code, animals.

You could plan ahead to link in with the annual Safety Week organised by the Child Accident Prevention Trust, which usually happens in June. This event will give you a source of leaflets, posters and probably some local events that can involve workers and parents together with the children. Definitely give the children an opportunity to voice their views about the following issues.

- How adults approach safety with them. In what ways do the children think you could improve the safety message? Do they think you fuss too much and explain too little?
- Older children may have some clear views about the ways in which adults could act in more safe and sensible ways themselves.
- Children are sometimes concerned about adults' behaviour, especially the people they care about, such as their parents smoking or not taking care of themselves.
- Children are more likely to listen to your warnings and concerns when they experience you as an adult who will also listen to their worries about you.

Further reading

Department of Education and Employment (1996) *Improving security in schools*, The Stationery Office.

Hillman, M., Adams, J. & Whitelegg, J. (1991) *One false move: a study of children's independent mobility*, The Policy Studies Institute.

Lindon, J. (1998) *Child protection and early years work*, Hodder & Stoughton.

Lindon, J. & L. (1993) *Your child from 5–11*, Hodder & Stoughton.

McConville, B. (1997) 'Happy campers', *Nursery world*, 16 January (a description of the Bridgwater Forest School).

Miller, J. (1997) *Never too young: how young children can take responsibility and make decisions*, National Early Years Network.

Playlink, HAPA & RoSPA (1997) *General guidance on health and safety on adventure playgrounds, a briefing paper*, Playlink.

Rawlings. A. (1996) *Ways and means: conflict resolution, training, resources*, Kingston Friends Workshop Group.

Troyna, A. (1998) *Providing emotional support to children and their families after an accident: guidelines for professionals*, Child Accident Prevention Trust.

Useful contacts

CAPT (the Child Accident Prevention Trust)
18–20 Farringdon Lane, London EC1R 3HA
tel: 020 7608 3828
e-mail: safe@capt.demon.co.uk

The Forest School
c/o The Children's Centre at Bridgwater College, Bath Road, Bridgwater, Somerset TA6 4PZ
tel: 01278 455464
e-mail: froodn@bridgwater.ac.uk
website: www.earlyexcellence.org

HAPA (the Hurtwood Adventure Playground Association)
Pryor's Bank, Bishop's Park, London SW6 3LA
tel: 020 7731 1435

Kidscape
2 Grosvenor Gardens, London SW1W ODH
tel: 0207 730 3300
e-mail: kidscape@dial.pipex.com
website: kidscape.org.uk

RoSPA (Royal Society for the Prevention of Accidents)
353 Bristol Road, Birmingham B5 7ST
tel: 0121 248 2000
website: www.rospa.com